MAKE IT OR BREAK IT;

STAINED GLASS FOR BEGINNERS

By

Phillip C. McKee, III

Award Winning Stained Glass Artist &

Retired Arlington County Firefighter/EMT

Defenders of the Pentagon

With Downloadable Projects and Trial Software

i

TABLE OF CONTENTS

PROLOGUE

Congratulations on purchasing this book and on venturing into the world of stained glass art. Stained glass is the only art form that is both revealed by light and transforms it as well. In two dimensions it draws a simple picture of colors bounded by lines of lead. But in three dimensions, it sculpts the very light itself and alters all of its surroundings. You are now well on your way to learning the exciting and fun art of stained glass as a hobby. Handmade stained glass panels, suncatchers and other art objects make for the most memorable gifts. And who knows, you may even transform it from hobby to career and begin taking commissions from friends, families and others.

This book is divided into lessons. Each lesson has a specific purpose and builds on all of the lessons before it. Don't be tempted to skip lessons or jump ahead. You need to do each lesson in turn so that you understand all of the concepts. If you do this, and don't move ahead until you've mastered the skills in each lesson you will in the end be able to make stained glass panels, windows and even three-dimensional objects. Of course, being able to make stained glass from pre-designed patterns isn't the last stage of this artform. You will one day want to be able to make glass of your own design. So, of course there will be a lesson on design basics. Each lesson will be structured in a particular way. I'll start by telling you the goal of that particular lesson.

Then I'll introduce you to the tools you will need for that lesson. Next you'll given a list of supplies and materials you will need to successfully complete these tasks. Some of these items you will absolutely need if you are to perform the lesson while other items are optional but will make your work easier. However, all of them are my best picks for your workshop.

At this point let me state I have not received any compensation of any kind from the producers or vendors of the items I recommend. These are truly my favorite picks for quality and performance for products. None of them have paid to be in this book, period. I refuse to take paid endorsements. Once you know what you'll need then the lesson proper will begin with instructions and images to help you along step by step. Finally, you'll be given a link to an online video against which to measure your understanding. Just keep at it. And remember, you can always turn to my website at *www.mckeestainedglass.com* for advice and technical tips. And let me remind you once again, don't move on to the next lesson until you have successfully completed the previous one. If you can't do one task, you definitely won't be able to do the ones that follow.

Finally, I've included three appendices to this book. The first appendix is a collection of easy to create patterns to get you a started on making stained glass. You'll find a set of sun-catchers, panels, door & window inserts, & three-dimensional objects that you should be able to make after mastering the techniques in this book. Some are easier than others. At the end of each lesson I'll list which patterns you should find yourself capable of making using the skills you've learned up until that point. Each pattern includes any tips or hints that might make it easier on you. However, all of these patterns are designed for the beginner. Later books will discuss more advanced techniques and will include patterns of greater difficulty. The third appendix includes information on where to download digital copies of the patterns and how to get a free trial copy of GlassEye 2000, an absolutely amazing computer-aided design program for stained glass.

Lastly, this book is meant for your enjoyment. I want you to have all of the enjoyment and fulfillment that I have felt and still feel from working in stained glass. This is a wonderful, if expensive, hobby and can also be a fulfilling line of work. If you ever have any questions or comments just go to my website at *www.mckeestainedglass.com* and share them with me. I will try to reply as time allows.

So go on, jump right in with Lesson 1 - Tools of the Trade and lose yourself in the wonderful world of stained glass.

Your Humble Teacher,

Phillip C. McKee, III

LESSON ONE - GETTING STARTED

Okay, now it's time to begin. The first thing you need to know is where to get your supplies. If you have a stained glass supply store near you that is probably the most convenient location although it will not always be the least expensive. To find such a store check your local yellow pages under arts, crafts, art supply & even under glass. I've found listings for stained glass stores in each of these categories depending on the publisher of that particular Yellow Pages.

However, for some people, especially those in rural areas, there may not be a stained glass supply store nearby. Even many urban areas have only one or two. For example, there are only a handful in the entire Washington, DC, metro area. Also, many of the local stores are very expensive. While it is nice to support local businesses, if you are on a budget that can place stained glass out of your reach. For either logistically or financially challenged readers the best place to shop is online. There are many different stained glass supply web sites. I would like to introduce you to mine. It is located at *www.McKeeStainedGlass.com* and not only offers a full line of stained glass, hot glass and mosaic supplies, but it also has a gallery of my work.

Okay, so now you've got two ideas of where to go to get your new toys. But the big question arises - What should you get????? If you go to almost all of the stores, both local and online, they'll have package deals where you can get the different types of tools and accessories in one bundle. So let's go over all the tools & supplies you will need to get started.

1) **Safety Glasses**: Yes, safety always must come first. You can get a good pair of safety glasses anywhere. In fact you can probably get them cheaper at your local home improvement or hardware store than you can at a stained glass shop. Just make sure they fit your face comfortably. If you can, see if the store will let you them on. Some people prefer the goggle style with an elastic strap around the back of their head. Some people prefer the traditional glasses style. Which ever you prefer, just make sure that it provides both front and side protection from flying glass. If it looks good on you that's an added bonus.

2) **Glasscutter**: Now, you can't have flying glass without a glasscutter. Contrary to popular belief and its own name, the glasscutter does not actually cut glass. Glasscutters are small tools that have either steel or carbide wheels on them that score a line on the surface of the glass. You then break the glass along the line using other tools and hence create the flying glass. As I said, glass cutters come in two main types, the traditional steel wheel and the carbide wheel. To keep the cutting wheel working you must always have it properly lubricated with cutting oil. Steel Wheel cutters have to be dipped in a small jar of cutting oil before each score. Most Carbide Tipped cutters have oil reservoirs in their handles and self-lubricate. Carbide Tipped cutters also come in several styles. The two most common styles are the Pencil Grip and Pistol Grip but there are also other variants such as the Toyo Thomas Grip or CustomGrip SuperCutter. This is just a matter of personal preference -

which shape fits your hand best. The biggest difference is that the pistol grip allows the user to apply pressure more easily and so tends to be popular among those with less grip strength or with arthritis.

There are several brands of cutters. My personal favorite is the Toyo line of cutters. The reason for this is that Toyo offers a larger variety of cutters so it is easy to find one that fits your particular grip and cutting style. Toyo also uses an innovative oil feed system. Most carbide wheel cutters with an oil reservoir feed oil to the wheel using a wick. It is a simple, effective and time-tested system. However, there is no way to effectively stop the wick from transporting oil to the wheel when you are not cutting. This means that a cutter with a wick can leak oil and can overfeed oil to the wheel. The only effective way to control leakage in a wicking cutter is to use a cutter cap. A cutter cap is a little rubber cap that slips over the top of the cutting head to contain leakage and protect the cutting head from damage. Some brands of wicking cutters are more leaky than others. For example, the Fletcher-Terry cutters use a wick that is virtually leakless. Toyo has an innovative and unique system that is simply light-years ahead. It has a valve activated system. When you press down to cut, the wheel assembly actually shifts backward slightly against a valve which releases controlled amounts of oil onto the wheel. Thus oil only flows in the precise amount needed, and only when cutting. I personally use the Toyo CustomGrip Supercutter.

3) **Cutting Oil**: If you plan to cut glass you have to have cutting oil. There are many manufacturers of cutting oil. Just make sure that the oil you buy is specifically designed for stained glass cutters. Also, you use only a very small amount of cutting oil at any one time so a small bottle will seem to last forever. I personally love the Inland Rinses Off brand.

4) **Running Pliers**: These can be rather difficult for some people to understand. Occasionally you will want to cut a long line, either straight or gently curving, in your glass. That's where these come in. You score your glass and then place the running pliers at one end. Metal running pliers have special plastic coated ends (which many people think look like duckbills). One is convex and the other is concave. The convex part faces up making it look like a frowning duck when viewed head-on. Many have small black lines marked on them to show you what part of the plier to line up with the score. You then simply squeeze the plier and the glass breaks along the score line. Instead of duckbills, plastic running pliers have a small dot and a notch. The dot is on the lower jaw and the notch is on the upper jaw. When you squeeze the cutters, the dot pushes the score into the notch and breaks it using the same general principle as the duckbills. Whether you use a pair of metal running pliers or plastic running pliers is up to you. Metal running pliers feel more substantial in your hand because of weight, whereas plastic running pliers are lighter.

5) **Breaking Pliers** (Optional): Breaking pliers look like plain old regular pliers. They have two square flat tips. You use them to grab onto a piece of glass and break it off the main section along the score line. This helps shape the glass into its final form before grinding. Most artists and hobbyists no longer use simple breaking pliers and I'll tell you why soon.

6) **Grozier** (Optional): Groziers are another form of pliers. They have two curved ends and serrated edges. They are used to groze or take "bites" out of the glass around the edges and further refine the shape in places where you just can't get a score line because it's too small. Once again, most artists no long use stand-alone groziers.

7) **Combination Breaker-Groziers**: This is why most people no longer use stand-alone breakers or groziers. These wonderful little tools have one curved side and one flat side. Both are serrated. To break glass you simply hold the flat side up and break as you would with a pair of breaker pliers. To groze the glass you use the curved side up. It combines two tools into one. Now, breaker/groziers come in many different sizes. As a beginner you can get away with having just one standard sized model. But as you progress you will probably want to buy a narrow-nose set to help with those tight corners.

8) **Marking Pen & Regular Pen**: The marking pen is a simple dry-erase pen or Sharpie. You can get this anywhere, though you can get them cheapest at an office supply warehouse like Staples or Office Max. Buy a bunch at once. This is what you will use to mark your glass so that you can keep track of which piece is which until you solder them together. You'll also need a regular old pen for marking your pattern. When you are working on dark colored glass, the Sharpie won't show up well enough. This is when you use a White Marker. These come in two styles. One is a white paint pen, and the other is a white Liquid Paper pen.

9) **L-Square**: Some people know this as a drafting square or a carpenter's square or even a speed square. Whatever you call it you'll need it for making 90° angles and straight cuts on your glass. However, make sure to buy one that is designed for use with glass. It will have special lip on it that the others do not. My favorite is the Rulex because not only does it allow you to do 90° angles but it is adjustable so that you can also easily repeat odd-sized angles needed for certain traditional grid patterns or other geometric designs.

10) **Flux**: Flux is an acid. It comes in paste or liquid form. You paint the flux on the joints you wish to solder together. Without the flux the solder won't run properly and won't stick to metal framing. After you are finished soldering you clean the flux off. For beginners I recommend Liquid Safety Flux. It cleans off with soap & water or window cleaner & a paper towel. Most importantly it is non-toxic (unlike many other fluxes), is safe to leave on your project over-night instead of requiring immediate clean-up, and it releases no fumes! For those who want the easy clean-up but prefer paste fluxes I usually recommend Aquaflux by Rectorseal. Regular fluxes are not water soluble and so require special chemicals called flux cleaners to remove. Many regular fluxes also contain toxic chemicals so make sure to read the labels carefully before purchasing.

11) **Flux Brush**: This is a standard acid brush that has corrosive resistant bristles and a metal handle. You can get them at any hardware or home improvement store in small bundles or online in bulk. Nothing fancy, just something sturdy with which to apply your flux. You can also use special liquid flux applicators if you have chosen a liquid variety

12) **Flux Cleaner & Scrubber/Scruffie**: You will also need to buy flux cleaner and a small scrub brush. Flux cleaner is a special soap that is formulated specifically to help remove flux and other chemicals from your piece. My personal favorite is CJ's Flux Remover. Even if you are using Safety Flux, CJ's will make cleaning a lot easier. The Scrubber is simply a small scrub brush with plastic bristles. Remember to scrub gently so that you don't break the glass but be thorough and get all the flux off. Flux is an acid and will corrode the solder lines leading to discoloration over time.

13) **Copper Foil**: As a beginner you will start by learning the Tiffany copper foil technique of making stained glass. This is actually a bit harder to learn than the lead came technique you see in large church windows because your cuts need to be more exact. However this means that when you later move on to lead work you will find the transition much easier than if you had learned the techniques in reverse order. Copper Foil is also less dangerous (not as much lead exposure) and it is the technique you must use when making 3-D objects like boxes or lamps. Finally, it is also not as messy as lead came.

Copper foil comes in many sizes. The larger the piece of glass the larger the foil width you should to use. Now the glass will remain the same thickness it's just that more foil will be showing after you wrap it around the glass. You want this because the more foil showing the stronger the solder joint and the more support the glass gets. You can use smaller foils on small pieces of glass for a more delicate appearance. The basic foil size that you should get as a beginner is 7/32" width foil. This usually comes in bags of 36 yards. Believe me; you'll use all of it. It never fails to amaze me how much copper foil is used on a single project. Just remember that the foil has to go around the circumference of every piece of glass in a project. You'll use lots of foil. Copper foil also comes with three types of backings. On clear or semi-clear sheets of glass you can see the backing through the glass. The first backing is plain copper. Hence you'll see copper through the glass. The other two are black-backed or silver-backed. Here it is just a matter of personal taste. If you plan on coloring the solder with a patina (either copper or black) then you'll want to use a copper foil with a matching backing. If you want to leave your solder lines the natural silver color then you would use silver backed. So, to start off you'll want to buy 3 bags of 7/32" copper foil, one of each backing. Venture is the brand of foil that I recommend. One note though, don't open the bag unless you plan on using it again soon. Copper foil will oxidize and lose its ability to stick to the glass. If you do have left over copper foil, be sure to put it back inside a sealable bag to protect it from humidity in the air.

14) **Patina**: There are two main types of patinas, Black & Copper. Both are acids that change the silver color of the foil to their respective colors. This is for artistic effect only and also only affects the outermost layer of solder. If you don't like the look you can always just scrub the solder with steel wool and try again. One important note - to use patina; pour a small amount in a little bowl. Paint the patina on with a Q-Tip. Then throw away whatever is left over. NEVER put used patina back in the bottle, as you will ruin the whole bottle. And never pour patina in the lid and work from that supply. When you recap the bottle, you can contaminate the patina just as much as if you had poured excess back in the bottle.

15) **Soldering Iron**: This is one of your most important tools as a stained glass beginner. If you get a low quality iron, you'll regret it forever. I have a very specific recommendation. Get an Inland Temptrol iron. It might seem expensive but it is worth the money. It has a built-in rheostat to maintain a constant temperature while still allowing you to adjust the temperature to suit your particular soldering needs. Cheaper irons you either have to keep plugging and unplugging to keep the right temperature or buy a separate rheostat (temperature controller).

16) **Soldering Iron Stand**: The bad thing about many irons is that they either come with a puny piece of bent metal to use as a soldering iron stand or no soldering stand at all. To protect your self, your work space and your project from the heat radiated by the soldering iron while it's plugged in but not actively being used you need a good soldering iron stand. My

favorite is made of nearly indestructible cast-iron, can be bolted to your worktable for permanent mounting (no accidentally knocked over irons) and it has a built in sponge which, when sopping wet, can be used to clean your soldering iron tip while soldering.

17) **Rheostat/Temperature Controller**: If you have chosen to purchase an iron without a built-in method of controlling temperatures then you will need to buy this as well. It is essentially a specially designed dimmer switch which controls the flow of electricity to your soldering iron and thus the maximum temperature of the iron. Stained glass temperature controllers almost always come with markings from 1 to 10 on the dial. If you are using a standard 100w iron then they will correspond to 100° to 1000°. It is important to note that under a certain setting the iron will not heat at all. Most soldering will be performed around the 7 setting. All irons are different so you will need to fine-tune your settings. If the solder doesn't melt well, raise it slightly; if the solder stays liquid too long or flows through from one side of the piece to the other, lower your setting. Decorative soldering (to be discussed later) is done on lower settings so that the solder will hold the decorative shape better.

18) **Solder**: Solder is what holds your stained glass projects together. It comes in several varieties - 50/50, 60/40, 63/37 and Lead-Free. These numbers refer to the respective amounts of tin & lead in the product. 50/50 is obviously an even mix. 60/40 has 60% tin and 40% lead. 63/37 is 63% tin and 37% lead. And Lead-Free solder should be just what the name implies, however some cheap solder manufactured overseas that is labeled as Lead-Free is actually a 97/3 mixture. Fewer and fewer people are using 50/50 solder. It has the highest lead content and because of that it is banned in many states (such as Pennsylvania). It also requires that you work at a higher temperature than the other solders.

I prefer to use traditional 60/40 solder on most flat panel projects because it is very strong and polishes to a higher gleam than 50/50. I also use 60/40 for three-dimensional work. 63/37 melts faster and at a lower temperature but cools quicker than does either 50/50 or 60/40, so it is perfect for decorative applications. Finally, Lead Free is the best option if you are worried about lead exposure for small children or if you are making an item that is to be handled frequently (like a jewelry box). If you do work with lead-based solder, don't worry; as long as you don't start eating the solder you shouldn't have any problems with the lead. Lead can only hurt you if you inhale the vapors or get the substance into your system. The temperature of your soldering iron is enough to liquefy but not vaporize the lead. And believe me; you will know if any of the liquid solder touches your skin so contact time will be miniscule. Solder comes in spools and the price changes as the price for raw materials changes. Buy the spools several at a time. I buy mine by the case and consider stocking up when the price is low. Not only is it less expensive to buy in bulk but you will use lots of solder, sometimes multiple spools in a single project. I prefer Canfield solder for its purity and soldering characteristics. It can be more expensive but it's worth it. One final note - do not buy solder at a plumbing supply or hardware store and think you're getting a good deal. The solder used for plumbing work is very different chemically from the solder used for stained glass. You will ruin your project over few extra bucks. Only use solder specifically manufactured for stained glass.

19) **Glass Grinder** (Optional): After you cut your glass you will need to grind the edges smooth. This keeps you from cutting yourself and it also keeps the glass from slicing up the copper foil as you apply it. Once you have done most of your shaping with the breaker/grozier, the grinder can help you finish off the piece. For a hobbyist just getting started I would

recommend the Inland Wizling. It is one of the most affordable grinders out there at around $100 at time of printing. I personally use the Inland Wizard IV. But remember, this is optional. Before grinders there was an old-fashioned way to get smooth edges.

20) **Carborundum Stone/Glass Stone**: This is the old fashioned method of smoothing glass edges. It's simply an abrasive stone that you rub along the edges to smooth them. It takes much longer than a grinder but it also only costs about $5 at time of printing.

21) **Fid or Lathkin**: It's a funny name for a simple product. Fids are little sticks that you use to press the copper foil firmly against the glass after wrapping. This process is called burnishing. You also use the fid to stretch open or press closed the slots on metal framing or lead came. Fids/Lathkins come in either wood or plastic. If you're not going to start doing lead came work soon after learning the basics of copper foil, then the rear end of your marking pen works just as well as a burnisher.

22) **Cutting Surface**: This is a special plastic board with hollow cells built into the surface. You cut your glass on this board and it catches most, if not all, of the small glass pieces also ensuring that your glass is level while scoring. Once you are finished cutting you simply shake your cutting surface/board over a trash can to dispose of the glass shards. The two most popular of these surfaces are the Waffle-Grid system and the Morton Surface system. Waffle-Grids are uniform 1 foot by 1 foot squares that are designed to be able to interlock to create cutting surfaces of any size desired. Morton Surfaces come as either Mini-Surfaces or Maxi-Surfaces and cannot interlock. Their set size can be convenient for easy set-up but can also make it difficult if you are working in an odd-shaped work area or one that is slightly too small for these larger cutting

surfaces. Both systems use exactly the same sized cells so that tools designed for one brand will work on both systems with only minor adaptations if any.

23) **Homasote Board**: This is something you can get at your local lumber yard. It is simply a type of pressed paper board that is often used by designers to create bulletin boards. You'll be using it as a layout board. Laying out your pattern will be discussed in the next chapter but it is important that your layout board be dense enough to support the weight of your project, soft enough to allow you to use push pins on it, and fire-resistent enough to hand soldering on it. Homasote board is the perfect product for this role. Some stores label this as low-density fiberboard.

24) **Morton Layout Block System**: This is a system of metal bars and push-pins that you can use to create perfect squares or rectangles when making panels. It helps keep your projects in their proper shape, especially if you plan to place them inside a pre-manufactured standard sized frame. The basic set comes with ten 6 inch blocks and 40 push pins. It can handle projects up to 16 inches by 26 inches. There are also expansion sets.

   a) Four 12 inch, four 3 inch & 40 push pins
   b) Two 17 inch and 16 push pins
   c) Two 23 inch and 16 push pins.

25) **Pattern Shears**: These are special three bladed scissors that you use to cut out your patterns. You'll learn more about them later but let's just say that without them it is infinitely more difficult to make stained glass. There are different shears for copper foil, lead came, and mosaic work. The gap created by the third blade allows for the addition of either foil,

lead or mortar between your pattern pieces without the overall pattern increasing in size.

26) **Double Bladed Pattern Knife**: This is an alternative to the pattern shear. These pattern knifes are hobby knives that have a special chuck which holds two blades instead of one. The chuck separates the blades the distance necessary for our work. Each knife comes with one chuck for copper foil work and one for lead came. One manufacturer is ProEdge.

27) **Glass Finisher**: Glass finisher is a product that cleans off the last bits of gunk from the glass and polishes both the glass and the solder with or without patina to a high shine. You just apply a few drops of this milky substance (always shake well before use) and then polish it with a smooth cloth (an old sock works nicely) just like you're waxing your car. When the film disappears you are left with a shiny finished piece of stained glass. For those who do not wish to deal with a liquid polish a great substitute is Nevr-Dull, a jar of cotton wadding that has been infused with polish. One nice thing about Nevr-Dull is that it can be used on many other surfaces in addition to glass and solder.

28) **Glass**: No glass project can possibly exist without glass. I recommend that you go online and buy a value pack of glass. These usually contain random assortments of a particular manufacturer's glass, though they are sometimes themed around a specific color or event (i.e. a July 4th pack of red, white and blue glass). It is usually much less expensive to buy glass in this manner for a beginner and it is a great way to build up a reserve of glass at home from which to choose as you are working. You can also buy glass by the sheet but this is usually much more expensive.

29) **Finger Saver Tape** (optional): Finger saver tape is plastic-empregnated gauze that you wrap around your fingers to protect them while you are

cutting, grinding and foiling. The tape is not adhesive but the plastic sticks to itself. So if you wrap the tape around your finger several times it will stay in place. Personally I don't use product, but years of violin have left the tips of my fingers with calluses that even sharp glass can't hurt!

30) **Bandages**: I don't mean to scare you but it's a simple truth, you work with glass and you are going to cut yourself. Even if you take every possible precaution, you will still cut yourself sooner or later. It just happens, especially right before or during grinding/smoothing. Get used to it. Once your finger tips develop calluses it will hurt less and less. Most cuts are just superficial little slices, like paper cuts, but because the finger tip is so full of little capillaries they'll bleed like anything. Always keep bandages handy because you don't want any of the chemicals you'll be using getting near the cuts. If you think lemon juice is bad, you've never felt a cut that touched flux.

31) **Rubber Gloves**: This is another simple safety product. The Flux & Patinas are acids. If you have even the smallest cut and get some inside, it will hurt like you just stuck the cut into fresh squeezed lemon juice and then decided to salt it down for good measure. When working with the patinas it is a good idea to wear a simple pair of yellow latex household cleaning gloves. These are reusable and available at your local grocery store or supermarket. You can also use medical examination gloves, but be sure to buy nitrile or other latex free gloves. More and more people are allergic to latex and don't know it.

32) **Towels**: You will need an abundant supply of cheap kitchen style towels as well as paper towels in your workshop for various stages of the process. I often use Scott Shop Towels because they come in huge rolls inside an easy to store and use cardboard dispensing box. They are far

stronger than standard paper towels but also disposable so they can be used in pretty much any situation where a towel is needed. This can be found in most hardware stores, home centers & auto parts stores.

33) **Glue Stick**: To glue the pattern to the glass for cutting.

34) **Sal Ammoniac**: Sal Ammoniac is a fancy way of saying Ammonia Salt. It comes in a solid white brick usually weighing 1/4 lb. It is also called a tinning block. If your iron is very dirty, or if it needs to be retinned, or if you are just done working with it for the day, it is a good idea to clean the iron tip using Sal Ammoniac. To do this, jab the iron tip (while still hot) into your flux for only a second. Then bite a tiny amount of solder off the roll and proceed to rub all of the edges of your iron on the Sal Ammoniac. Repeat these steps until your iron tip is the same nice, shiny silver that it was when you first purchased it.

35) **Light Box** (optional): A light box is a box that has a light source on the inside and a large piece of white glass or plastic on one large side to act as a diffuser. The diffuser makes sure that the light from inside is evenly spread throughout the surface of the box. Light boxes also often have a mirrored surface on the interior of the side opposite the diffuser to increase the light output and to aid in diffusion. You use a lightbox to assist you in telling just how a piece of glass will look when under full lighting conditions. It can also be helpful when determining glass grain (more on that later) and when trying to do a final fitting on your pieces. If you decide to get a light box, I recommend one that uses the TrueLight system as that most closely mimics the spectrum of light emitted by the Sun.

Those are the basic items. In later lessons, other specialty tools and supplies will be introduced as the need arises. Now I know that this list seems intimidating, but you can get great deals on kits from many places. You can also go to my website to order one of my beginner kits and get everything you need and more at a fair price.

Okay, now that we've gone over basic materials let's talk some more about safety. Working with stained glass is not only an expensive hobby it can also be a dangerous one. There are numerous safety rules that you must follow to make sure that this is a safe and enjoyable hobby. First, set up your workshop in a location that is well ventilated. There may not be any lead fumes but there will be fumes from the flux. Also, if you move on from copper foil to lead came then you will have lead dust in the air as well. Therefore it is important to be in a room with windows you can open during nice weather or where you can install a ventilation system. Second, set up your workshop in a room with a flat, smooth floor. Glass will shatter if dropped and small shards of glass will break off as you are cutting, especially when you are grozing. If your workshop has carpet you will find it very difficult to clean up the glass shards from the floor. Third, never use a regular household vacuum to clean up your workshop floor or work space. Only use a vacuum that has true HEPA filtration for vented air. Otherwise you risk stirring up lead dust should you be using lead came. Fourth, never work in an area where food is prepared or eat/drink in your work area. This is especially important if you are working with lead came because you can create lead dust that you don't want to ingest.

Fifth, ALWAYS and I mean ALWAYS wear your safety glasses while you are in your workshop. Even if you are just moving a piece of glass from one table to another or walking around with your creation there is a chance you could drop it or bump into something and send glass flying. No hobby is worth losing an eye. Sixth, whenever you are working with patina, always wear gloves. Remember, patinas are mild corrosive agents and can burn your skin, especially if you have any exposed cuts. Seventh, bandage cuts immediately and keep them covered until they are fully healed. Most people only wear a bandage for a short time. When working with glass it is vitally important that you keep all of the chemicals and lead away from open wounds. Eighth, always wear shoes in your workshop and don't allow children or pets into that space. It may sound like common sense, but neither you nor your children or pets will want to cut their feet on glass shards. Also, shoes will keep drops of molten solder from burning your toes. Ninth, try to have a work smock or lab coat that you wear or maybe an apron or some other garment that is only used for stained glass work. This will keep any chemical spills or lead dust off your regular clothing. Also, only wash this work outfit with towels that you will be using in your workshop. Don't wash it with your other clothing. There may be glass or lead dust on it and the last thing you want is to one morning find a piece of glass in a sock or underwear. Finally, only keep your soldering iron plugged in when you are going to use it and always keep it in its stand even when not in use. A hot soldering iron is hot enough to set paper and/or wood on fire. So it's also a good idea to have a smoke detector and fire extinguisher in your workshop just in case.

You can also visit *http://www.monkeysee.com/play/5783-how-to-make-a-stained-glass-suncatcher* to watch a video of the preceding information as well.

All right, we've gotten the safety points out of the way and you've set up your workshop. The next thing to talk about is glass. Not all glass is alike. There are numerous manufacturers and each one has something that makes them unique. Even within the line-up of one manufacturer there can be variations. There are many different ways to divide glass into types. The first great division is between float glass and art glass. The glass you find in a standard household window or at hardware superstores is float glass. This is a clear glass that has cooled while floating on a pool of mercury. In this way it is perfectly smooth on both sides. It comes in a variety of thicknesses. Single-strength is the size used for picture framing. Double-strength float glass is thicker and has breaking and cutting characteristics most similar to art glass. It's not the same, but it's as close as you can get without buying art glass. Because of mass production techniques, float glass is much less expensive than art glass and so is the perfect glass to use when learning and practicing how to cut glass. Art glass is any glass made using a rolling technique and that has had color or colors, texture and/or opal added to it. Art glass is more expensive than float glass and is harder to cut. Unfortunately, the most beautiful hand-rolled glasses are also the most expensive and the most difficult to cut for use in stained glass.

Another way to categorize glass is by how it is made. It can be machine-rolled or hand-rolled. Machine-rolled glass is gathered, mixed and then rolled entirely by machine and is therefore of uniform thickness and usually has a smooth surface on both sides. It also usually has a greater uniformity between sheets than does handrolled. A classic example of this is Spectrum glass. Hand-rolled glass has been gathered and the colors mixed by people using large iron rods. After the colored gathers have been mixed it is then pressed through a set of rollers that are hand cranked or machine assisted. It is also sometimes pressed using a single table mounted roller which moves along the sheet as it lies on the rolling table. Either way this produces a glass with more variations in color, thickness and surface texture. It will even have small air bubbles trapped inside. These are not imperfections but part of what makes hand-rolled glass so beautiful. A subset of hand-rolled glass is Antique glass. This doesn't mean that it is old glass; just that the glass was made by the old techniques. In this case, the gathered glass is blown into a mold so that it forms a cylinder. Once it is a cylinder of the desired size, the ends are cut off and the cylinder is sliced lengthwise. The cylinder then unrolls on its own into a single sheet of glass. However, as it unrolls it is also cooling, so the glass develops small lines crisscrossing the surface. These lines are the hallmark of Antique glass.

Yet another way to classify glass is by light transmission. This creates a division between Cathedral and Opalescent glass. Translucent glass which is a single color but allows as much light as possible through of that color is called Cathedral glass. Some people will erroneously refer to it as colored clear, but clear glass should only be used to refer to actual clear glass like that used in standard windows. Cathedral glass is the traditional glass used in stained glass windows and is what you see in the medieval windows of Europe. It is still the primary glass used in European stained glass artworks.

However, during the late 19th century, American stained glass artists were looking for something to fulfill their artistic ambitions. They wanted a glass which not only colored light but captured it. With Cathedral glass, the light passes through the glass and colors what lies beyond. It looks gorgeous in transmitted light, as long as you are standing on the opposite side of the glass from the light source. However, if you look at a window made out of Cathedral glass from the outside on a sunny day, it will appear to be uniformly gray. That is because Cathedral glass transmits too much light and does not reflect enough light back at the viewer outside. Hence it looks bland under reflected light. American artists wanted glass which would look equally good under both transmitted and reflected light. What was developed is called Opalescent glass, though Europeans still often refer to it as American glass. According to the US Patent and Trademark Office, the inventor of opalescent glass was Louis Comfort Tiffany, the great giant of American stained glass. And so it is that history records Tiffany as the creator of an entire school of stained glass design and manufacture. However, obsessive-compulsive historians, like me, will point out that even though Tiffany was given the patent on the glass, LaFarge - the much too often ignored genius and contemporary of Tiffany - used opalescent glass of his own invention in a window that predates Tiffany's application and the date Tiffany claims to have invented the manufacturing technique! However, it was the technique that Tiffany developed which was popularized and was adopted by manufacturers, not LaFarge's. So no matter who actually did it first, it was the Tiffany method that is still with us today.

By mixing various colored glass with opal, Tiffany was able to create a glass whose ability to transmit light was controlled and which looked just as good under both transmitted and reflected light. It also could have much greater complexity of color. Instead of a sheet being a single color, opalescent glass can have as many colors as desired by the manufacturer swirled together. Each color does not loose its distinctness but instead coexists beside each other in a symphony of light. Opalescent glass doesn't transmit as much colored light so it does not create the colored pools on the floor that characterize Cathedral glass. Instead it seems to capture the light within itself and burn with an inner fire. Most importantly, it obscures the light source, so it was the perfect glass for lamps, screens, or for wealthy patrons wishing to block out the ugliness of the newly industrialized world and instead see idealizing images of nature or of our mythic past.

Not all opalescent glass is of uniform opacity. Some allow more light through than others. For example, there are some glasses that are totally opaque and are used primarily in mosaics. While others - such as wispy or Spectrum's Baroque Glass - actually mix a Cathedral or clear glass with slight wisps or streaks of opalescent.

One last way to divide glass into categories is by texture. It can either be untextured or textured. "Untextured" does not mean perfectly smooth. Both smooth machine-rolled and bumpy hand-rolled are considered untextured. "Untextured" simply means that the natural surface that the glass acquired during the manufacturing process has not been intentionally altered. Most textured glass has had a roller with a three-dimensional pattern pressed over the sheet while it was still hot. This roller then creates a continuous, unbroken pattern along the entire surface of the glass. Textured glass can be either machine or hand-rolled. While the texturing process is mechanical, the method of turning the glob of glass into a sheet is what determines whether the glass itself is hand or machine-rolled. But because most textures are applied using a roller, the designs for the textures are usually copyrighted unless they have been in use so long that they are now in the public domain. As such, each manufacturer of textured glass has, for the most part, a unique line of textures. Spectrum, Kokomo, Pilkington - these are just a few of the fine companies making textured glass. There are far too many available textures to go over each one. Instead, I'm only including the most commonly used and commonly available textures that a beginner is likely to encounter. These include many of the classic textures that are made by multiple manufacturers.

The most common texture that a beginner is likely to encounter is Glue Chip glass. It is also one of the most beautiful and on of the few textures that is not created with a roller. Glue Chip is cathedral or float glass that has had one side etched to create a frosted surface. Animal hide glue is then applied to the frosted surface and allowed to dry. The glue then gets a good grip on the microscope peaks and values of the etched surface. At this point it is then baked in an oven or kiln to 500º. This baking causes the glue to break apart into scales and then peel up at the edges. As it curls up, it pulls off pieces of the etched surface. Where it remains on the glass, the surface keeps the etching; where it has peeled off and taken glass with it the surface becomes clear again. After it has baked enough, the glue and glass scraps are cleaned off. What is left is a feather or frost like pattern on the glass. You can find almost any color of Cathedral glass imaginable in glue chip. And there are also crystalline animal hide glues that you can mix with water and apply to etched glass at home to create custom glue chip glass. Double glue chip has had the animal hide glue applied twice but is only etched once. Corded glass has a textured side that makes it looks like a bunch of cords loosely lying beside each other. Next is drapery. This looks like drapes on a window, there are even folds in the rough side of the glass. The glass has literally been folded in on itself. Drapery glass can be very difficult for the inexperienced glass cutter because of these natural lines of weakness and extremely uneven thickness of the glass.

English Muffle glass is made by Wissmach and is a glass all its own when it comes to texture. It has a semi-translucent appearance of a single color and a wonderful mottled effect in light transmission. Glass similar to this was extremely popular during the Victorian period immediately prior to Tiffany's opalescent revolution. Granite has a rippled appearance. Hammered takes this effect to the extreme. This glass looks like it has been hammered flat by a thousand tiny little hammers each leaving their own little strike-mark.

In this book I have coined a new term for a particular texture. That is "aqueous" glass. I use the term aqueous because there are several manufacturers who make a glass that looks as if the top of a gently rolling pond was captured and turned into colored glass. Water Glass is the Spectrum Glass Company variety, while Kokomo calls theirs Wavolite, and it has still other names given it by a few smaller manufacturers. Aqueous glasses are one of the most gorgeous glasses out there - a truly beautiful glass to work with especially when trying to make water or atmospheric effects. Seedy has hundreds of small bubbles trapped within the glass. In fact it looks almost like the dying gasp of a drowning man. These bubbles, also found in other types of glass, add tremendous beauty and character to glass but also make it more difficult and unpredictable for beginners to cut. Seedy is another of the textures that does not involve a roller. Rainwater is a Spectrum product that has small humps of glass on one side so that the glass appears to have rainwater cascading down the surface.

Krinkle glass is one that always grabs people's attention. It has the appearance of paper that has been roughly crumpled into a ball and then flattened out once more. But when you touch it, it makes one think of alligator scales. Quarter-Reed was chosen here to represent reeds of all sizes. This is extra thick glass that has a series of perfectly straight, parallel, semi-circular channels cut out of one side. If you look at it on edge you see a series of half circles equally spaced all in a row. The space in between the channels is still flat with sharp edges. There is no smoothness to this as there is with rippled. While the channels and spaces are uniform on any single sheet, manufacturers offer different types of reeded glass with different sized channels and spaces for each type. This glass was extremely popular during the Art Deco period. These channels do make grinding and foiling more difficult. The final glass is more of a surface treatment than a texture.

Fractures & Streamers is one of the most beautiful glasses around. Embedded on one side are hundreds of small, paper-thin pieces of broken glass called "fractures" and long thin lines of colored glass (either straight or bending) called "streamers." The manufacturing of this glass has not changed appreciably since it was invented by Tiffany himself. First bubbles of colored glass are blown over a large metal collecting basin. Once these bubbles have been blown to a size where the walls are of a miniscule thickness, they are broken off and allowed to fall into the basin. Because of their extremely thin surfaces they cool thoroughly during their short descent and shatter at the bottom of the basin. These "fractures" are then scattered across the rolling table. Next, long thin strands of colored glass are pulled to the desired thickness and bent into the shapes desired. These "streamers" are then also placed on the rolling table. Finally the base glass, usually but not necessarily clear or white opal, is placed on the table and rolled flat. Because the fractures and streamers are so thin they immediately reheat and fuse to the cooling glass base.

Finally there are some chemical surface treatments that I should mention before we move on - iridized & dichroic glass. Once again we return to the genius of Louis Comfort Tiffany. During his career, Tiffany was exposed to Roman glass that had been unearthed at archeological digs in Syria. This glass had been buried for almost 1000 years in soil that was high in metallic content. Over the centuries, the metals had migrated into the outer layers of the glass, creating a shimmering iridescent effect on the surface. Tiffany loved the look of it, but didn't want to wait as long as it took nature to create it. So he invented a technique of spraying on a metallic coating that created the iridescent effect on one side of the glass sheet. This is called iridized glass. Almost any type of glass can be iridized, from cathedral to clear to opalescent. Even textured glasses and glue chip are often produced with an iridescent effect on the smooth side.

Dichroic glass is a much newer invention. It actually came to glass art as a dividend from the space program. It manages to have a different color depending on which way you look at it. It is created by using "thin film physics" or color separation. Now we definitely don't need to go into the physics of how it's done but a brief explanation of the practical technique is in order. Manufacturers of dichroic glass take regular glass, usually clear or black, and make sure that it is absolutely clean. It is then placed within a special vacuum chamber that also is a furnace. Once inside, metallic oxides (titanium, silicon, magnesium and others) are placed in a crucible before the temperature is raised to 300 degrees. The oxides are then vaporized by an electron beam and redeposit themselves on the glass in layers less than 3-5 millionths of an inch! Each oxide is placed as a different layer, and some are coated multiple times, 40 to 50 coatings are not uncommon; the amount of each coating and the order of the coatings determine the exact colors that will be reflected by the dichroic glass. The coatings create this effect by allowing some light to be transmitted and some to be reflected depending on the angle at which the light impacts the glass. However, dichroic glass can be difficult to work with because the coating is much easier to scratch off than that on iridized glass. Dichroic glass is especially popular among fusers and glass jewelry makers.

There are many other specific textures and types of glass but space keeps me from discussing them all. However, there is one more thing to say about both textured glass and hand-rolled glass before we go any further. For any kind of glass other than Spectrum or float glass, there will be a rough side and a smooth side (or at least a smoother side). You can determine this by rubbing your fingers along both sides. For most textures it is very easy to figure out which side is smooth and which side is rough. But for some very expensive hand-rolled glass, that will be harder to determine as both are rough to different degrees. For these glasses, you need to determine which side is smoother. The reason you do this is because we always cut glass on the smoother/smooth side.

Also, practically every glass except clear float glass and some machine-rolled cathedral glass has a grain. By grain I mean a pattern of irregularities or color that creates a linear pattern in the glass. This is very easy to see in wispy or streaky glass or in textures that are linear such as quarter-reed glass. In some glass it is not as easy to see (such as on complex textures or highly colored opalescent glasses). One way to figure out the grain is to take two sheets of the exact same glass. Hold them up to a light or place them on a light box so that you can really see the details of the glass. Note how they look together. Now rotate one sheet 90 degrees. In one configuration, the lines and colors of the two sheets will line up. In the other they will appear to be at right angles to each other. It is best to mark you glass by drawing an arrow with your sharpie (since sharpie ink simply washes off glass) to indicate the grain direction. This will become very important later one.

You can visually review the different types of glass by viewing the video at *http://www.monkeysee.com/play/5784-understanding-the-different-types-of-stained-glass*.

Now you know about your tools and you now about glass. The first practical thing we are going to do is to learn how to score. Grab your glass cutter in your hand as is appropriate for that style of cutter. For steel wheel cutters, most people either attempt to grab it like a pencil or grasp it firmly in their hand with their forefinger resting on the slight widening of the metal near the head and the thin body of the cutter between the first and middle fingers. If it is self-lubricating make sure that the oil well is properly filled. If it is a steel cutter first take a folded up paper towel and place it on top of the open bottle of cutting oil. Rapidly turn the bottle and towel upside down and then right side up. This will create a wet circle of oil on the toil. Before making a score with a steel wheel cutter or other non-self-lubricating cutters, be sure to roll the cutting wheel through the oil on the towel. You may have to rewet your towel several times during the course of your work.

Now, take a piece of inexpensive double strength clear float glass that you can easily purchase at most window glass shops or home-centers. If your bargain box came with a piece of plain, un-textured clear glass then you can use that piece instead if you prefer. Take your glass cutter and touch the wheel to the glass at the edge but not on the edge of the glass. The sharp edge of the glass can actually take a bite out of your cutting wheel and ruin it so it is important to start and stop your scores just barely inside the actual edge of the glass. Press down with a 45° angle between the back of the cutter and the glass and keep the angle between the sides of the cutter and the glass at 90°. Never allow your cutter to lean to either side as this will lead to a poor or nonexistent score.

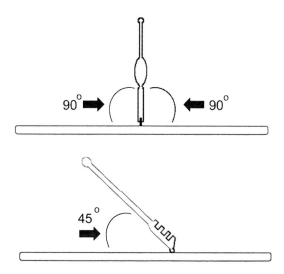

Now push the cutter forward all the way across the glass along the center line of the sheet in a straight line and lift up before you roll off the far edge. Always push away from yourself. You want to see where your cutter is going, not where your cutter has been. Never roll off the edge of your glass as that will do the same thing as starting on the exact edge.

You should have heard a screeching sound while you scored the glass. That is the sound of a score being made. Not all glass will make that sound but most will. You should also see a fine line on the glass. If there is no line, then you didn't press hard enough. If the line appears chalky then your cutter needs more oil or a replacement wheel. If there seems to be small flecks of glass on either side of the score or you actually saw glass flying off the score as you made it, then you are pressing too hard. If the glass shatters while you are scoring or cracks in an odd way, then it is most likely not on a level surface. Another thing to note, never score a line twice. You should also never cross an unbroken score line with another score. Running your wheel over a previous score before breaking it can ruin your cutter. Going over a score is just like going over the edge of the glass sheet. If the score didn't come out the way you wanted just break it and try grozing or grinding it to size. However, always remember this "Shape to Grind, don't Grind to Shape," as my mentor taught me.

Now line up your running pliers with the score. The score should be placed exactly in the center of the pliers' jaws when the side of the pliers with the adjustment screw is facing up. If you are holding it properly, when you look down you should be able to trace an imaginary line down the score and straight down the handles of the pliers without any bends. Hold the running pliers with your forefinger between the handles near the fulcrum. That way, if you squeeze the pliers too hard, you'll know because of the pressure on your finger, long before the glass shatters. The screw on metal running pliers is supposed to allow you to avoid this practice but since glass can vary in thickness, especially hand-rolled glass, the old finger method is actually more useful. Be sure to only hold the glass with the pliers. Do not hold either side of the glass with your free hand as it can alter the break. Instead place your free hand under the score so that you can catch both pieces of glass if they escape the grasp of your pliers after the break. Now gently squeeze the handles until you hear the glass snap.

Congratulations, you've now made your first glass cut. If your glass cracked along a line different from the one you scored, take a close look at the glass. There might be a natural flaw in the glass that could have caused the problem. If so, the break will veer off the score at the location of the flaw. It might have also been that you put too much pressure, especially if the glass just shattered in all directions. Most commonly it was simply a poor score. However, more than likely you have a nice, pretty, clean line down the center of your glass sheet. If not, then just try again until you get it right.

You can review cutting a straight line by watching the video at *http://www.monkeysee.com/play/5785-how-to-score-and-break-straight-lines-in-stained-glass*.

Now, lay the clear sheet of glass over the top of the last page of this lesson and copy the symbols at the end of this lesson just as your see them onto your glass using your marking pen.

These are the steps that you will be following when you cut any piece of glass:

1) **Liberate** - Score and cut a line to separate the piece you are working on from the rest of the glass. If a score breaks poorly, there is no reason to ruin your entire piece.

2) **Start on the most difficult side!** - There will always be at least two sides to any pattern piece you are cutting out. Usually there will be more. Always start with the side that is going to be the hardest to cut. This will make sure that you don't waste time on the easy cuts if you have a bad break on the difficult one. It will also help make the difficult cut easier, especially if it is an inside curve. (More on that later) You will then continue to the next hardest side, and so on, until you have cut all of the sides.

3) **Groze** - If you have any little knobs are sharp pieces of glass that are sticking out of your outside curves, groze them to remove the knobs. You will learn how to groze in a few paragraphs.

4) **Grinding** - Once you have gotten your glass as close as you can possibly manage by hand to the final shape, then you grind it the rest of the way. Grinding both brings out the details of the piece and it also smoothes the glass edges.

Cut lines between the shapes and break them using your running pliers so that each shape is on its own piece of glass. Now, score a line along the long edge of the rectangle (piece #1) from one piece of the glass all the way to the other. Grab the rectangle with one hand and the breaker/grozer with the other, flat side up. Use the same grip as with the running pliers by placing your forefinger between the handles near the fulcrum. With your free hand grab the piece of glass that you are going to use so that you can hold it firmly while placing your forefinger parallel to the score but not on the score so as to buttress the glass. Next grab the glass with your breaker/grozers on the other side of the score with the flat side of the pliers facing up and the pliers' handles lined up perpendicular to the score near the midpoint of your score. Once again, grab near the score but not on the score. Now break the glass as if you are snapping a pencil in two. It should have broken off along the score line. Do that same process for each of the other four sides. You should have a nice little rectangle ready for grinding/smoothing. Now try the triangle (#2). It should be done the same way as the rectangle.

Now move on to shape #3 - the circle. It's a little more difficult but not much. A circle is just long convex line (outward bowing). This is more commonly known as an outside curve. In this case, there is nothing but an outside curve. You cut this by scoring a series of straight lines along the edge at tangents. Score and break each one in turn until you have a rough approximation of the curve. The little knobs can be taken off by grinding or grozing. If the knobs are large, you should try to groze them first. To do this, flip your pliers over so that the curved side faces up. Now, grab the piece of glass you are going to keep firmly with your free hand. Then take your breaker/grozers (curved side up!) and bite down on the little knob that you don't want. While applying pressure pull your pliers away from the glass on the horizontal plane. If you were biting hard enough, then you should have pulled off the knob and leave a rough edge on the glass. You can then grind the remaining roughness away using either your grinder or a grinding stone once you have finished the other cuts. (You will learn how to grind in the next chapter.) Always remember, for outside curves you score one tangent, and then break it. Only after it has broken along the score do you make another score!

You can watch the outside curve video at *http://www.monkeysee.com/play/5786-how-to-score-and-break-an-outside-curve-in-stained-glass.*

Let's review quickly. First we liberate. That's when you cut out the piece from the main sheet of glass so that if you make a mistake it won't affect any other piece. Then you do the hard cuts first because that's where you are most likely to mess up. If you do mess up while doing the hard cuts, just move the shape to another piece of glass and try again.

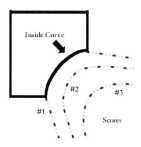

Okay, now for the hard part, concave (bowed in) curves. This is what is called an inside curve. Piece #4 has two inside curves and two straight lines. Normally you would select the deepest inside curve to cut first. Each of these inside curves is the same, so simply choose one. Now you need to start scoring. For an inside curve you will score several curves one after another, each one inside the last. One will be exactly along the curve you want to break. Then score a series of curves exactly parallel to it and in the same shape but about a centimeter (half inch) away from each other until you reach the edge of your glass. In the diagram the piece you want to keep is drawn with a solid line and the scores are dashed lines. The first score you would cut would be #1. Then you would score line #2, and finally line #3. These are called relief scores. You will score all of your relief scores before you do any breaking.

Now start breaking off the pieces starting with the furthest from your final break, in other words in the reverse order in which you cut them. Make sure you are grabbing the main piece between the break you are currently breaking and the next one in the series. Before you try to break it though, you need to weaken the score. The reason for this is that glass naturally wants to break along the shortest, easiest path. The curves you have just scored are neither. So, to get it to break on that line you need to create micro-fractures in the glass along that score line.

There are three ways to create these micro-fractures. The first way is what I call the "wiggle." To do the wiggle, grab the glass as if you were going to attempt to break along the score. But instead of actually breaking it, just lightly jiggle the breaker/grozers up and down. By doing this you are tapping the flat side against the glass and creating those imperceptible micro-fractures. And don't just do this in the center of the break. Start at one end of the score and work all the way over to the other end. That way you create them all along the score.

The second and best way to create micro-fissures is by truly tapping along the score and is actually the most common method. To do this take your glass cutter and hold it by the cutting end (the side with the wheel). Now hold the glass firmly with your free hand so that it doesn't bounce with each hit. Place the cutter under the glass so that the ball is lined up with the score. Now begin tapping upwards so that the ball is striking the glass directly beneath the score. You will hear the tapping noise. Work up and down the score just as you did with the wiggle. With this method you will not only create micro-fractures but, if you do it right, also create actual cracks along the score line. If you hold the glass to the light and look at it at an angle from underneath you will be able to see the cracks forming (for all glass except very opaque opalescent glass). If you have a good ear you will also hear a tonal difference in your tapping once cracks start to form. The glass will sound one way where the glass is still solid and then note will go flat as the crack is formed.

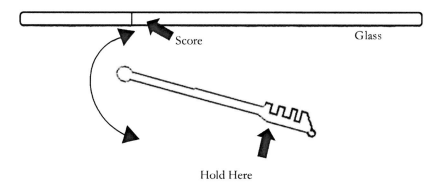

The final method of creating micro-fractures is actually breaking off one of the outer scores! So once you have weakened score #3 and then broken it off, you have actually created micro-fissures in both scores #2 & #1. So by the time get to #1 it will already have micro-fissures in it even before you begin wiggling and/or tapping. So the more relief scores you create, the easier it will be to make your final score break properly!

After a score is weakened, grab it at the midpoint of the score and attempt to break it as you did for the straight lines with your breaker/grozer. If it doesn't break easily, try to create more micro-fissures. Sometimes, the piece will actually break off while you are trying to weaken the score! If only a part of the score breaks off, simply move your breaker/groziers over to the new midpoint of the remaining score and try to break it again.

Inside curves are very tricky so I highly recommend reviewing the video of this process at *http://www.monkeysee.com/play/5787-how-to-score-and-break-an-inside-curve-in-stained-glass.*

If you had cut the flat sides before attempting the inside curve, then when you tried to make the final break you would most likely break the score badly and snap off the small extensions at the top and bottom. However, by leaving the glass intact on the flat sides for now, you have created a safety zone. The shortest distance to an edge is now longer through the pattern piece and so the break will most likely follow your score. This is another reason why you should always do the easy straight lines last.

If you do this procedure right you will wind up with a piece with only the two easy side cuts left for you to cut. If not, copy the piece over and try again. Now try shape #5. Use the lessons you learned on how to break inside and outside curves to do the S shaped sides first. Start with the inside curves on each side. Then do the outside curves on each side and finish it off with the flat sides. Finally, for a real challenge you can try to cut out shape #6.

Congratulations, you've cut your first set of glass pieces and you've learned all the basic hand cuts that you will use throughout the rest of your life in making stained glass. Now to smooth the edges; if you bought a grinder, follow its instructional manual on what to do. If you have a glass file slowly rub the file along the edges of your glass until they are smooth. Now put these aside as keepsakes, your first pieces of cut glass.

Finally you can review all the stops by watching *http://www.monkeysee.com/play/5788-cutting-out-a-stained-glass-shape.*

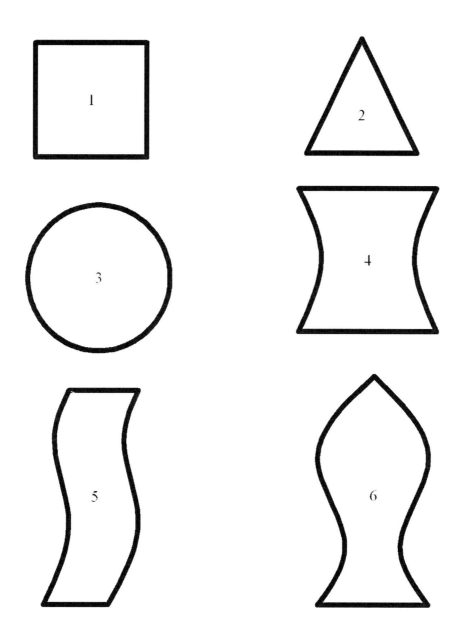

LESSON 2 - YOUR FIRST SUNCATCHER

Tools & Supplies Needed: Glass, Pattern Shears, Homasote Board, Morton Mini-Surface, Morton Layout System, L-Square, Marking Pen, Glasscutter, Running Pliers, Breaker/Grozer, Grinder or Glass File, Lathkin, Copper Foil, X-Acto Knife or Hobby Razor, Foiling Tool (optional).

Okay, now you are ready to try your first suncatcher. Look for "Pattern #1" in Appendix 1. It is the first pattern. This pattern will use all of the different cutting skills you learned in Lesson 1. Make 3 photocopies of the pattern. There are multiple reasons for this. First, you will be learning how to make stained glass using the "American Pattern-Cutting" method. There is also the "English" method. You actually already used this method. In the English method you place the glass over the pattern and trace it using a marker as you did in the last lesson. For colored glass you usually put both pattern and glass on top of a light box to assist in seeing the pattern through the glass. Unfortunately this can be very inaccurate. You have to be certain that your hand doesn't waver from the pattern as you trace. Then you have to be certain that you know whether to cut along the inside or the outside of the traced line or your pattern size will be off. Finally, you have to remove the exact amount necessary to leave space for the foil or lead by eye. You have to know how far away from the exact pattern line you really need to cut. Getting a consistent gap by this method is extremely difficult for anyone other than a very experienced professional. Even for experienced artists, this can lead to extreme variance in solder thickness and to poor overall appearance in copper foil work. I do not recommend the "English Method" to any beginner.

In the pattern cutting method you will have one pattern to use as layout, one to cut, and one to use as a spare. It is important to make them all at once because there is a little known feature in modern photocopying machines. Photocopiers don't actually make a perfect copy in the exact same size as the original. When doing a 100% sized copy a photocopy machine actually increases the size just a tiny amount to make sure that there is no black line around the edge of the copy created by the edge of the paper. This size increase varies by brand and model of copier. So if you have to make a spare copy later you may find that the size of the pattern pieces aren't the same as the original copies!

You will tack the layout pattern down to your homasote board and the other will be cut in pieces to guide you as you cut your glass. The other reason that you always make two photocopies at the same time is that photocopy machines don't actually make an exact copy. They enlarge the item slightly so that there is no accidental black line around the copy. This might not sound like much but it can totally throw off a glass pattern. You always want both patterns to be made at the same time so that the magnification will be the same for each copy. If you want to be extra safe, make even more copies.

First take one of your photocopies and place it on top of your homasote board. Then, place a layout block exactly along the bottom edge of the pattern. Have the side of the block with holes touching the homasote board and facing away from the pattern. You want the flat unbroken side forming a vertical wall at the pattern's edge. Make sure a small amount (about 1/4" to 1/2") sticks out past the left lower corner of the pattern. Use at least two tacks to hold this block in place. Be sure to push the tacks in all the way otherwise the block will be loose and move around. Next, put your L-square against the bottom block and line the side of the L-square up with the left side of the pattern creating a 90-degree angle with the existing block. Now tack another layout block in place along the pattern edge. Use one more tack to hold the upper right corner of the pattern in place. You have created a level work surface and a right angle to guide you as you assemble the suncatcher. You will begin assembling the suncatcher in the corner that is bounded on 2 sides by layout blocks and work your way towards the open sides of the pattern.

Confused by how to place the layout blocks? You can always see how it's done by watching *http://www.monkeysee.com/play/5791-laying-out-your-stained-glass-pattern.*

Next, place your other photocopies next to the first. Take out your pen and number all of the pieces, using the same number for each piece on each copy. This way, after you cut the second pattern apart you know where it goes on the original. This isn't as important on a simple pattern like this one but it is invaluable on larger more complex projects. When you are making a window with 500 separate pieces and you don't number them, not only will you have the challenges of stained glass but also the challenges of a jigsaw puzzle.

You also will write down on each piece of a paper a code to designate what color it is supposed to be. For example, all the pieces you want to be blue could be marked with a B; all the pieces you want to be Red could be marked with an R, etc. Finally, if you are using glass that has grain, such as ripple or wispy, you will want to put an arrow showing the direction you want the grain to be going. Grain is that sense of direction that appears in almost all glass, even machine made glass. Sometimes it is created by the way the colors seem to flow in a mixed color sheet. Other times the grain is created by the physical shapes and layouts of textures on the glass. Either way, you want to be certain to control the grain direction in your piece. If you will have several pieces of the same glass in a creation, you will normally want all of the grain going in the same direction so that they appear a part of a larger whole. This is especially important for backgrounds, like sky. You can also use grain to show motion. If you are putting a tree in your artwork, you can line the glass grain up with the tree limps and trunk to make it look like this is a living tree and that the grain is the actual bark flowing along the growing form.

Once you have finished labeling each piece, the layout pattern, the cutting pattern and your spare pattern should have 3 things written on them - number, color & grain direction. At this point, either on a blank spot of your layout pattern, write down what each code means. If you are using 6 different shades of blue in an artwork and you stop working for a while, when you start back up on the project you might not know which shade is B1, which is B2 and so forth. Always have a written decoding table to allow you to know what color goes where. It's a good idea to copy to decoding table onto the spare pattern as well, just in case.

You can review this process at *http://www.monkeysee.com/play/5790-going-from-a-paper-pattern-to-a-stained-glass-pattern-piece.*

So, let's review. You've got three identical photocopies of your pattern. You've tacked one down to the homasote board and created two sides of a border using the Morton Layout blocks and the L-square. You've also labeled all patterns with your three pieces of identifying information. The next thing you do is to take a regular pair of scissors (or a paper cutter for straight lines) and cut along the periphery of the cutting pattern. Next, take your foil pattern shears and cut the first piece out of the cutting pattern. It is a good idea to only cut out one pattern piece at a time. This helps you avoid losing pattern pieces. Notice how the pattern shears take out a thin 1/32-inch line of paper between the two sections. This is to take into account the thickness of the copper foil that you will be wrapping around the glass. But we'll get to that later. For now, just know that the little strips of paper can be thrown away but that you need to create those little gaps between pieces for your project to fit together properly after foiling. If you do not take into account the thickness of the foil your pattern will either grow or simply not fit together at all. I recommend to my students that they start working in the corner that is squared off by the Morton Layout Blocks. Then continue along one of the squared sides. Finally, cut the rest of the pattern. This helps you monitor potential growth caused by cutting pieces too large.

After you cut out one piece of the pattern take it over to the sheet of glass that matches the color. Rub the glue stick on the back of the pattern and place it on the glass so that the arrow lines up with the grain of the glass. Cut out, glue and paste only one pattern piece at a time. If you cut all of your pattern pieces at once, you run the risk of losing pattern pieces especially if you do not have a permanent work space. Also, glue and cut only one pattern piece from your glass at a time. If a glued pattern piece stays on your glass for too long, you may find that the glue is difficult to clean off your glass later. When placing the pieces onto the glass it is important to glue the pieces far enough away from each other so that they can be separated from each other before final cutting but close enough together so that you have spare glass left over to use in case you mess up any piece on your first try at cutting it. Believe me; bad breaks will happen even to the most experienced artists.

That is why God made spare glass. In addition, do not glue pattern pieces directly at the edge of your glass. It may seem like this will save you from making some cuts, but it will actually make the remainder of your cuts more difficult, especially if those cuts are inside curves. Inside curves have a bad habit of breaking bad at the edges, and extra glass will help protect those points from damage. The diagram shows a properly placed pattern piece well away from the edges of the glass and with proper labeling. This piece has an inside curve, is the first pattern piece, is on blue glass (B) and has the arrow aligned with the grain.

Once the pattern piece is glued down it is time to begin cutting. First use straight lines and your running pliers to separate the pattern piece from the rest of your glass. Normally your pattern piece will be much smaller than the actual sheet of glass. You want to first liberate the smallest area possible around the pattern piece from the rest of the sheet. Often this can be

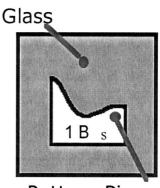

accomplished with just a straight line across the sheet or by a diagonal line. That way a bad break on one piece won't mess up the rest of your sheet. Also, keep in mind where you would like to place the rest of your pattern pieces on the glass. If there is a particular effect in the glass you wish to use, don't damage it or leave it on an edge during liberation. You might also have multiple pattern pieces of similar sizes but different shapes. You could then liberate one long strip of glass and further break it down into multiple smaller liberated areas for each pattern piece.

Be sure to hold your glass over the cutting surface while you are doing any breaking that way the little cells will catch the small glass shards and make clean up easier. Now begin using the techniques you learned in Lesson 1 to cut out all of the pieces and form them to their approximate shape. Pay special attention to the bowed in sections/inside curves. The pointed parts at the top are easy to accidentally break off. As you cut out the pieces lay them in their approximate place on the pattern. Don't worry if they don't fit perfectly yet. If there are sharp points or large amounts of glass left, take your breaker/grozer pliers and hold them so that the curved side is facing up. Now use them to bite off excess pieces of glass. This process is called grozing and is used to chip the piece down to the closest possible approximation of the final shape. The edges will not be smooth, and the shape will not be perfect after grozing. That is what grinding is for. Now, here is where personal preference comes in to play. Some people like to cut out all the pieces of a single color before moving on to the next color. Other people like to cut out the pieces in the order in which they appear in the pattern, starting in one corner and then moving out. Also some people like to rough cut all their pieces first and then grind them all at once. Other people like to cut one piece, grind it and then move on to the next. Any of these approaches is okay. Just find the one that fits you. However, I recommend that you begin with the piece in the squared off corner and move out from there. This will allow you to easily see if your pattern is growing due to systematic errors in cutting and also allow you to compensate for any errors in cutting more easily.

Grinding is an important step at this point. You need to be very careful how you handle the freshly broken glass. The edges will be especially sharp. This is the moment when you are most likely to cut yourself. If you are using a glass grinding stone, very carefully, methodically and slowly rub the stone up and down the edges of the glass until you have moved all the way around. Depending on the file, you may need to keep it wet during this process. This will take some time so be patient.

If you are using a glass grinder then your life will be much easier. First, be certain you have set up your glass grinder according to the manufacturer's instruction. This will most likely mean filling up the water reservoir to the appropriate level and adding in grinder coolant. Once the grinder is properly prepared (a grinder head is in place and is being lubricated) then run each side of the piece across the grinding head quickly. This is just to get rid of the sharpest points. Hold the glass by placing your fingers on the top flat surface only and with sufficient pressure to move the glass around in a controlled manner. This will protect your fingers until you can safely hold the glass by the edges. Now, carefully run each edge through more slowly until each side is the proper shape. If there is a bump or protuberance that should not be there, just slide it back and forth against the grinder head with gentle pressure for a little longer and it will disappear. Don't hold any one spot against the glass for too long or you'll wind up with a round indentation in the side. Also, don't apply too much pressure, as this can damage the grinder's impeller shaft - the part that connects the motor to the grinder bit - thus rendering it inoperable.

This is where the temptation comes to get sloppy with your cuts and use the grinder to get the shape, pressing the glass against the grinder with constant, hard pressure and running it slowly along edges to take off lots of glass. This is a bad idea. It will cause excess wear on the grinder head & grinder motor and force you to change the water and grinder bits more frequently. Like my mentor told me, "Shape to grind, don't grind to shape." Do this for every piece. If you are relying on your grinder for shaping you can also find yourself grinding off too much glass and before you know it the piece will be too small for your pattern.

If you are using the glass grinder you will notice that the water will naturally loosen the glue and the paper will slip off. Once this happens, dry the glass piece and use your marking pen to write the number back on it. The other information is now obvious and doesn't need to be written down. If you are using the glass file you will need to use some water to help you get the paper off the glass and then mark it. Once the pattern piece has been ground, cleaned and marked put it in its final position on the layout pattern. The piece should fit the space perfectly. After you have done more than one pattern piece you will begin to see how the pieces fit together. They should fit cleanly with only a small space in between. If they don't, then look closely at the problem points. Find which piece is sticking out past its assigned area or overlapping another piece and regrind where necessary. You may even need to recut an entire piece especially if you have large gaps. Don't worry, what is important is getting all the pieces to fit together loosely within the outline of the pattern. Now repeat these steps for all the pattern pieces. As each piece is finished, check it against the layout pattern as you did before.

Once again, why should they fit loosely? Because the next step is foiling. The copper foil adds just a little bit of thickness to each piece of glass and without that extra space your pattern will grow as you foil it. That's why foil shears cut out that small strip of paper from between your pattern pieces. There are lots of different machines out there that claim to help you foil. Some are hand held gizmos that lay the foil down and then crimp it in place, but they must be moved around the piece of glass. Others are large machines that stand still but through which the glass is fed. Personally, I won't use any of the large machines but you may decide differently. However, the beginner should always learn hand foiling before relying on a machine.

Foil comes in copper backed, black-backed or silver-backed. You should use the foil with the color backing that you want for the final seam. Since we will be applying a black patina to this pattern, use black-backed foil. Foil also comes in multiple widths. The wider the foil the more will show around the edges of the glass and the larger the bead. Larger pieces of glass need larger beads to support them. For the beginner 7/32-inch foil is the best to use. But for artistic reasons you might want smaller beads on your artwork. Feel free to mix foil widths in a single work for artistic purposes. Just don't mix backing colors. There are even now specialty foils with scalloped edges to create a decorative, almost beaded effect. You can do the same thing by carving a wide foil after it has been applied, but for many people the extra effort is not worth the money saved.

Foiling is the process by which you carefully wrap the copper foil around a piece of glass and burnish it so that the adhesive holds the foil to three sides of the glass; the front, the back and the side. Solder is a metal and it will only bond to other metals. Without the foil you wouldn't be able to hold pieces of glass together. That's why in the old days they used lead came. Copper foil was invented by Louis Comfort Tiffany because you couldn't do three-dimensional work with lead came and foil allowed for more intricate patterns. Copper foil has an inherent strength that unframed lead came work doesn't. In some ways it is more difficult; in some ways it is easier. But it is definitely better to learn how to use copper foil first and more useful to learn how to use copper foil. While you can only make panels with lead came, you can make anything with copper foil: panels, windows, vases, boxes, lamp shades, sculptures, card holders. The list goes on and on.

Start by separating the end of the copper foil from the backing. At this point an optional copper foil holder can be useful. Somehow keep the foil and the paper backing apart. If you are using a multi-slot holder you can thread the paper back through another slot to assist you. Be careful to avoid touching the adhesive with your fingers as much as possible. The oils on your hands along with any dirt will interfere with the adhesive's ability to stick to the glass. Now, sighting down your nose, place the piece of glass in the middle of the copper foil. This will take some practice. Slowly wrap the glass with foil until the foil overlaps itself, keeping the glass centered on the foil the entire time. Always start and finish wrapping on an inside edge - a place where there will be glass on both sides of the foil - and not on an edge that will face the outside of the pattern, because at this location solder will completely encase the overlapping foil. That way, if after you are finished this weak spot in the foiling tries to come undone should the adhesive fail, then the solder will hold it in place. If it is facing the outside it can come off and ruin the whole piece. Applying the foil around the glass is actually more accurate, though less intuitive, if you think of yourself as applying the glass to the foil and not as wrapping the foil around the glass. By rolling the glass down the foil it is much easier to keep it in the center of the strip for uniform solder lines on both sides of the finished product.

As a beginner it is important to use machine rolled glass for its uniform thickness so that this part of the process will be easier. Foiling glass from Youghiogheny, for example, can be very difficult because it will be of varying thickness and rolling in shape. But this shape is created by the same hand blowing process which makes the glass so beautiful and wonderful to use in advanced artwork. In fact, when making a Tiffany Style Lamp, I often use only Youghiogheny glass. However, as a beginner you are best advised to use glass from Spectrum to take advantage of its shockingly strict uniformity.

Once the foil is wrapped entirely around the piece, use your fingers to press the glass down on the front and back of the glass. Do this using a pinching action. Pinch in one location, then move to an adjacent spot and do the same all the way around the piece. Never pinch and then attempt to slide your pinched fingers along the edge as the very thin foil can give you the mother of all paper cuts. In areas with inside (bowed in) curves slowly rub your finger along the flat, non-adhesive of the copper until the heat of your hand causes the thin metal to bend down naturally and not break during this process. If the foil does break it will create a pizza slice shaped wedge of an empty space. To correct this, just cut off an extra bit of foil and apply it perpendicularly to the original foil. Pinch and burnish it you normally would and thrim off the excess that hangs below the edge of the rest of your foil with your X-Acto knife.

After all foil has been pressed down use your lathkin to burnish or press down along all of the edges. Start with the sides and then press down on the top and bottom. This will ensure that the foil adhesive sticks to the glass. If the foil has been left out too long it can oxidize and not stick properly. Also, if the glass is still wet or has gotten oily the foil will not stick. In these cases just clean and dry your glass and try again. Wrap and burnish all the glass. As you finish burnishing each piece take a look at the spot where the foil overlaps itself. If the overlap is not exact, use your X-Acto knife or razor to trim off the excess and make the burnished foil on the front and back into a straight line. Once burnished and trimmed, then place them on top of the pattern. The wrapped pieces should fit exactly over the top of the pattern and with each other inside the outer edge of the pattern without significant gaps between pieces. Don't worry if it's not perfect. This is your very first piece after all.

Foiling is an extremely difficult process to master and perform consistently well. You want the exact same amount of foil showing on both sides of the glass AND you don't want any messy overlaps. So I highly recommend watching *http://www.monkeysee.com/play/5792-how-to-apply-copper-foil-to-your-stained-glass-shape* to make sure that you have all the concepts in place.

Since this is a square/rectangular piece you can now do something known as squaring the pattern. Get more pieces from your Morton Layout Blocks and place them on the remaining two sides of the piece. Once again, use your L-Square to ensure that you are creating 90° angles at each corner. Tack them in place so that all the pieces are pressed firmly but not too tightly against each other. You don't want the piece to buckle upwards, just to be held in place within the original dimensions of the pattern. This step is especially important later on when you are making large hanging panels that you wish to frame and are planning to use pre-manufactured frames of a particular dimension.

You can review squaring off at *http://www.monkeysee.com/play/5793-finish-laying-out-your-stained-glass-pattern.*

LESSON 3 - BASIC SOLDERING

Soldering is the process of melting a mixture of tin & lead onto foiled or leaded glass so that the pieces stick together. Your suncatcher may not yet be finished but soldering is a difficult process and deserves a lesson all its own.

Tools you'll need: Everything from Lesson 1 plus a soldering iron, soldering iron stand, temperature controller, wet sponge, solder (50/50 or 60/40), flux, flux brush, flux cleaner, cleaning brush, finishing compound, and several old rags.

Now, let us return to the serious business of safety. You will now be starting a process where the worst accident is not just a simple cut, but the potential for creating a severe burn or worse, a large fire. Soldering should be done with complete concentration and no distractions. If you are about to solder, make a commitment to continue on until you are finished. Don't stop and put down you iron to go answer the phone. Don't decide halfway through that this is the perfect time to rearrange the flowers on the living room coffee table. Now is the time to solder and nothing else. I speak from experience. I once allowed myself to get distracted and in reaching for the phone, passed the soldering iron from my right to my left hand. Only one problem, I was holding the iron handle with my right hand but when I passed it I gripped the hot soldering iron tip with my left. Needless to say I got a very severe 2nd degree burn from my moment of distraction, and the telemarketer on the other end of the line got an earful of profanity that would make a sailor blush. The other major safety rule for soldering is that if you are not holding your soldering iron in your hand then it needs to be in its holder. A soldering iron should never, I repeat NEVER, be placed directly on a table or work surface. The tip of the iron does reach temperatures that can ignite wood or paper and cause a fire. Also, though this should be self-evident, don't touch the tip to anything that you don't intend to solder. Finally, don't touch the melted solder until it has cooled and solidified. It will be just as hot as the iron at first and cause just as bad a burn. Always wear your safety glasses when soldering.

Okay, so now it is time to solder. Dip your flux brush into your flux and place small dabs of it at points between each piece of glass so that your pattern has a flux glob on every joint including the ones right next to your layout blocks. Now take your roll of solder. Unwind about a foot of it at a time. Take your soldering iron in your dominant hand and your solder in the other. Hold the tip of the solder just slightly above one of those dabs of flux, maybe a centimeter or half-inch above, with both of them directly over one of the dabs of flux. Now press through the solder with your hot soldering iron, set around the 7 on the temperature controller. This will grab a small amount of solder and deposit it on the fluxed joint. There will be some bubbling and hissing as the solder melts away the flux. This is supposed to happen. There will also be an awful smell. That's the evaporating flux and the reason why you want good ventilation. What you did is called "pressing through" in soldering terms. Later you will learn how to solder by "running the bead." Press through the solder at each point where you have placed flux. You should have a nice little pattern with all of these dots of solder when you are finished. Now make sure that all of the pieces of glass have a dot of solder on every joint. If they don't, then add it at this time. The solder around the outside edge joints is especially important as these will act as dams helping to keep your molten solder from flowing off the pattern in the next step.

You can now take off all of the Morton layout blocks and tacks. If you did, grab your suncatcher and lift it off the paper. It will already be stiff enough for you to move it around, lift it up, or even flip it over. However, for our purposes we have done this simply to allow you to rotate the pattern piece as needed during the next stage of soldering. Hold your soldering iron so that one point just barely touches the end of a seam and the handle of the iron points towards the center of the pattern. It is very important that the iron hang over the pattern and not over the edge. Once the solder is hot the angled iron tip can act like a spout on a pitcher. If the iron body is hanging off the edge of the pattern it can cause the solder to flow off the pattern instead of along the foil. Also, do not put your iron tip directly onto the dam you created in the previous step. You want part of that dam to remain so that it can help keep your solder from flowing off as well. Press the solder against the soldering iron tip until you notice solder running off the tip and onto the seam. Slowly drag the soldering iron along the foil, making sure to deposit enough solder along the way to have a nice bead of solder sticking up above the glass. This is called "running a bead of solder."

Running works great when you have two pieces of glass that fit perfectly together. However, what do you do when you have a gap between two pieces? That is when you "float" solder into the void. Press through solder onto the void slowly with small pauses between presses. This will give the first press time to set up before it gets heated again. Remember you want the solder to fill the void not run out underneath the hole. Continue to press through until you have a nice flat level of solder totally filling the hole. Now use the press through method to add a small bead to the top of the floated void.

The aim of all of your soldering, whether you press through in a series of drops or float a void or run the seam, is to create a nice uniform bead of solder about 1/8 of an inch tall in the end. There will be times when doing three-dimensional work or decorative work that you will want a flat bead; or when you are framing you may need a flat bead just at the edge where the frame overlaps your panel; but, for the most part you will always want a small bead on all of your soldering work. Just remember, that right now you are only doing "rough soldering." Your first dots and beads will hold everything together and then later you will go back, reheat them and make the nice final appearance.

Because soldering is so important to the final appearance of your stained glass artwork, please be sure to watch the video at *http://www.monkeysee.com/play/5794-soldering-your-stained-glass-piece.*

It is personal preference whether you want to create solder lines by running solder along the seams or pressing through in a series of beads. I do both depending on the length of the line and proximity to an edge. Either way, once you have finished soldering all of the seams on one side of your suncatcher flip it back over. You will probably notice big bubbles of solder where it leaked through while you were floating a void. Don't worry, solder melts. After you paint the seams with flux, just go back to those bubbles with your soldering iron and press on them until they melt and form the beginning of a nicely beaded seam. Do the same thing on this side that you did on the other, either running or pressing along to create beaded seams.

If you ran your seams, where they join up there will be odd-looking meeting points. If you pressed through then you will have a series of small humps along the seams. Now is when you make your seams pretty - in other words, it's time to do "finish soldering." Slowly press your iron against each seam moving along a tip width a time so that the whole seam gets remelted and then solidifies again. If you ran your seams then you may only have to do this at the corners. This will give you a nice finished bead without noticeable joints or funny bubbles. If your solder starts to pull up as you lift your soldering iron then just add more flux to it. If bubbles form and then leave craters, too much flux is under the solder, just keep reheating it and letting it cool until it finally cools smooth. Just always make sure that you give the solder time to cool between reheats so that it won't fall through to the other side.

Once one side is finished off, paint a large amount of flux all around the outside rim of the pattern and then glide the tip of your iron around the edge of the piece. Did you notice that a little bit of solder will adhere to the copper foil changing it from copper to silver color? That is called "tinning." You want to tin the edge all the way around. If there isn't enough solder on your tip to get a whole edge, just tap the tip of your soldering iron against the end of your solder and then tin some more.

After one side is finished and tinned, flip the piece over and finish off the beads on the other side as well as tin the edges. Now is where a third set of hands or two sturdy objects (chunks of scrap wood, book ends, or best of all "Wedgie Jrs."). Use these "extra hands" to hold the suncatcher on its edge. Now tin one edge at a time until you have tinned all the way around.

Finish soldering gives that final, professional look to your soldering lines to be certain to review it at *http://www.monkeysee.com/play/5795-finish-soldering-your-stained-glass-piece.*

Finally it is time to add reinforcement if necessary. In this case it really isn't but we'll do it anyway just for practice. Take some 24-gauge wire. You can buy it pre-tinned from a supply store or online or you can get untinned wire from a hardware store. Solder the end of it to the spot where you want your hanger to be located. Now carefully bend the wire around the edges of your piece soldering at single points as you go just to hold it in place. Remember, you can't apply solder without first applying flux. Once you have gone all the way around and back to the beginning take the free end and wrap it a couple times around a pencil. Now press it back down against the edge and solder the hoop against the side of your piece. Then get your extra hands out again and begin applying a bead of solder along the edge to hide the wire. Be careful because the solder will want to just slide down the sides. Apply only a little solder at a time using the pressing method and let one spot cool completely before pressing down its neighbor. Once you have made a nice bead all the way around the wire will be totally hidden. You will also have already put in place a hoop you can use to hang it from a suction cup on your window.

Some people don't like a simple wire hanger or wire reinforcements. You can buy lead castings that work as hangers and that will attach to either the side or a corner. If you use a lead casting don't create a hoop with the wire. Instead solder the end down after cutting it to length and bead around the edge. Once you have beaded the edge, attach the lead casting by soldering it to the spot you have chosen. You can also frame your suncatcher using suncatcher thickness lead came or zinc channel, but those framing techniques will be discussed in a later lesson.

Think you're done? Wrong. Flux is a corrosive and if you left it in place it would slowly damage the glass and the solder lines. Get your flux cleaner, cleaning brush and take your suncatcher over to a sink. Squirt a small amount of cleaner onto the glass and scrub it with a wet brush. Once it is nice and soapy looking, wash it off in the sink. Do this for both sides. Later on when you are doing pieces too large for your sink I recommend getting a large bucket and a wet sponge for final cleaning.

Okay, the flux is off. It's time for the next step - Patination & Finishing. But before we leave soldering, let me reiterate one point that I learned when I was beginning. Never hurry through the soldering process. You will be far more pleased with your work if you take your time and do it right. Hurried soldering leads to uneven beads and bubbly surfaces, while patient soldering leads to consistent beading and a polished surface. Take your time and do it right. It is well worth it.

LESSON 4 - PATINATION & FINISHING

Tools & Supplies: Patina, cotton swabs, rags, finishing compound, household rubber gloves, piece of steel wool or copper scrub pad.

Once you have fully soldered and cleaned your piece it is time to decide what color your seams will be. On their own they will appear bright silver. For some pieces this is exactly the look you want. Other times it just doesn't go with the general tone of the piece. Your two main choices are copper colored or black. To get these colors you apply a patina to any surface that has solder. Patina is a corrosive so always wear rubber gloves when working with patina.

Take your bottle of patina. Make sure you use the same color as the backing of your foil. On clear pieces the backing will show through and it will look bad if the backing color differs from the seam color. First, take your scrub pad/scruffie and scratch the surface of the solder in all directions. These scratches will help your patina attain a much better appearance and will be invisible when you are done. Use only all steel or all copper scruffies, never plated. The plating process involves chemicals that can interfere with patina. Next, pour a small amount as your working supply into a clean cup/bowl.

NEVER work straight from the bottle or use the bottle top. Residue from your piece can contaminate and ruin your bottle otherwise. Use a disposable cotton swab, such as a Q-Tip, to paint the patina along the solder lines and edges of your piece while really scrubbing it in. The color will change before your eyes. If you see places you missed or that need more, then just paint more on. Be certain to get in along the edges between the solder and glass. New stained glass students can easily miss this area due to the shape of a cotton swab and accidentally create silver outlines around their patina finish. When you need more patina, flip the cotton swab over and dip the clean cotton into your working supply of patina - NEVER double dip. Do this all over the entire side. When you are finished and have the color you desire just wipe off the patina with a rag. If the color just didn't get strong enough for you, take the scouring pad or steel wool and rub the seams vigorously again. Wipe with a rag and reapply the patina. The second application will have a stronger, deeper color than the first. Do this as many times as necessary to achieve the desired depth of color. Once you are finished with one side, do the other. After you have done both sides throw away any patina left over in your working supply. Never put the used patina back in the bottle with the unused portion. This will contaminate and ruin your patina.

Finally there is finishing. Take your finishing compound bottle and shake it vigorously. When you squirt some out onto your project it should be milky in color. Now using a rag rub it in circles just like you are buffing a car. At first a smoky film will appear on your glass. Keep rubbing gently until the film disappears. Your glass and seams will now have a nice shine to them. Do this to both sides. If you are using Nev'R Dull, simply tear off a small piece of the wadding, rub into along the seams, and then buff as described above.

Congratulations, now you need only get a suction cup and hook from a craft store or glass supply web site and hang your newly completed suncatcher in the window. Now that you have completed your suncatcher it is time for something much more challenging, an entire panel.

A great video of the patination process can be seen at *http://www.monkeysee.com/play/5796-applying-patina-to-your-stained-glass-piece.* You can review the finishing process at *http://www.monkeysee.com/play/5798-finishing-your-stained-glass-piece.*

Now you're ready to tackle these projects:

1) Simple Caduceus
2) Easy Shamrock
3) Police Officer Thank You
4) Firefighter Thank You
5) Firefighter Teddy Bear

LESSON 5 - MAKING A HANGING PANEL

While it may seem like making a hanging panel is just a scaled up version of making a suncatcher it really isn't. There are many challenges unique to a hanging panel, especially when it comes time for framing.

Tools: 4 pieces of Glass, Pattern Shears, Homasote Board, Morton Mini-Surface, Morton Layout System, L-Square, Marking Pen, Glasscutter, Running Pliers, Breaker/Grozier, Grinder or Glass File, Lathkin, Copper Foil, X-Acto Knife or Hobby Razor, Foiling Tool (optional), Flux, Flux Brush, Solder, Soldering Iron, Flux Cleaner, Scrub Brush, Patina, Scruffie, Cotton Swabs, Finishing Compound, Rags, Framing supplies.

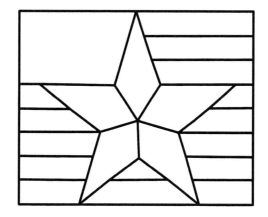

This is the panel that we will be making. It uses four different colors of glass but not too much of any one color so you should be able to get away with only one small sheet (8x10) of each color when you order it or get it from your supply store. All of the glass used is Spectrum to make it easy on the beginner.

The colors are (name & product number):

1) Cherry Red Cathedral Waterglass: S-151W
2) Steel Blue Cathedral Waterglass: S-5384W
3) Opal White: S-200S
4) Clear Cathedral Granite: S-100G

You can order by product number either from your local stained glass supply store or by going online. This pattern is intentionally simple because at this stage you will still be practicing your basic skills. Later on we will create a larger more intricate hanging panel.

To begin, go to Appendix 1 and find the pattern for Flag Star. Make three photocopies or printouts just as you did for the suncatcher and lay it out in the same manner. Cutting and foiling the glass and squaring off the glass are also the same as on your previous project, simply on a larger scale. Things get a little different when you get to the soldering. Before you solder you need to decide what type of frame you will use. Since this is a standard size (8x10) you could just get an off the shelf frame and replace the backing and glass that comes with the frame with your stained glass. This will look great from the inside of your house but you will see the unfinished back of the frame when you look at it from outside your home.

Your other two options are wood or metal channel. You can buy these at either your local stained glass supply store or online. These products are not usually carried by craft shops or by hardware stores. Wood channel comes in either 6-foot lengths that you cut to the appropriate size or in sets of two pieces pre-cut and pre-drilled of a certain length. In this case you could buy a large length of channel and miter cut it to the appropriate lengths, or buy precut wooden channels that fit the finished pattern.

Your other option is to use metal came. Metal came, such as zinc came, only comes in 6-foot lengths but it comes in different widths so that it won't look out of scale with the rest of your work depending on the size of your panel. You will always have to cut metal, but that doesn't necessarily mean miter cuts. Later on I'll show you an easy way to frame with metal that doesn't involve a single miter cut.

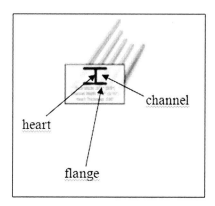

Every piece of metal came has three parts: the heart, the channel, and the flange. The channel is the empty space into which you insert your glass. The heart is the center, vertical support that holds the front and back of the came, is the back wall of the channel, and provides structural rigidity to the came. The flange is the metal that sticks out from the heart forming the side walls of the channel. It obscures the edges of your glass. There are also two main types of came: H and U. H channel has flanges that stick out on either side of the heart creating an H shaped profile (see image above). U channel only has flanges on one side creating a U shaped profile. U channel is primarily used for framing. H channel is used to join two smaller panels together inside of a single frame.

Whether you use metal or wood you need to measure the depth of your came channel. Most came channel is 3/8 inches deep. But some may be different. Always check, never assume. This number is important to know because for the length of the channel depth in from the edge all the way around your piece you will want to flat solder instead of beading your solder. So the nice bead won't start until 3/8 of an inch in on your piece. The reason is that most channel is just barely wide enough to hold the glass firmly and glass and bead will be wider than the channel. The last thing you want to do is finish your piece and find that it won't fit in the frame.

Wood framing with miter cuts is relatively simple. Just cut 45 degree angles, but be sure to measure your pieces from the bottom of the channel and not from the edge, otherwise your frame won't come out right.

If you are going to frame with metal channel and want to use miter cuts the steps are the same as for wood. But there is an easier way to frame with metal. First measure the width of the metal channel from its heart to its edge. Now, make a straight 90 degree angle cut on a piece of channel equal in length to your piece plus two widths of channel. Place that on the bottom of the piece. Now, measure from the edge of the channel to the top of your piece. Cut two pieces of channel equal to that length plus one channel width. Now measure the remaining piece of exposed glass and cut a piece of channel to that length. Notice that your frame now has perfect 90-degree angles at the corners and there wasn't a single miter cut involved. But we're not done yet. Use your pins to hold the framing pieces in place and then flux the joints where the pieces meet. Finally solder them together.

Soldering metal channel is slightly different than soldering your glass together. The primary difference is that the metal channel is a heat sink. The heat from the iron is absorbed by the metal and rapidly diffused along the entire length of the channel. This means that if you try to tack solder the corners the way you did earlier, the channel won't be hot enough to bind to the molten solder. To solder channel, you first need to flux the channel and then gently rub it with the soldering iron tip directly for a second or two. This will warm up the corner sufficiently to allow the solder to bind. Only after the corner has been preheated should you attempt to solder it together. The heat sink properties of the metal channel also mean that you need to be careful when handling a freshly soldered metal frame. Even though you were only soldering in the corner, the entire length of metal will be hot.

Now, use your extra hands from earlier and hold the frame on edge. The bottom piece of channel will have two holes at either end showing. Just use some solder to fill them up. There will also be two holes facing up at the top of your piece. Before you fill these, use something known as a Handi Hanger or use the wire-round-the-pencil trick to create two hangers, one for each hole. Place your hangers in the hole, flux it and then fill with solder. This will hold your hangers in place and hide the holes at the same time.

And that's all there is to making a simple hanging panel and framing it. However things get a little harder when you make a panel sized object that has an irregular shape or has more difficult cuts.

I recommend reviewing the process of making a metal frame at *http://www.monkeysee.com/play/5797-framing-your-stained-glass-piece.*

Now you're ready to tackle these hanging panels:

1) Granny's Fan Quilt
2) Welcome Sign
3) Star Cross
4) Bevel Cross
5) Star of David

LESSON 6 - IRREGULAR PANELS

In this lesson we will make two panels. One will still have 90-degree corners but will have more complex shapes in it and the other will be a free-form large window hanger. First the odd/complex shapes panel.

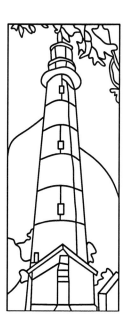

The purpose of this panel is to get you thinking about how to do more difficult cuts easily. You have had practice making simple cuts so far, now it's time to challenge yourself. This next piece is 6 inches wide and 15 inches tall.

Because of its length, you will have to be very careful at the step where you flip it over to solder the back side. The image is the Chincoteague Light House in Virginia. It is one of the most beautiful lighthouses in North America.

You will use ten different colors of glass in this sheet. You may decide that by now you are ready to try another brand and see how they break, but I recommend that you still stay with Spectrum a little bit longer before you move on to some of the more expensive glasses.

Here is your glass list:

1) Cherry Red Cathedral Granite - S151G
2) Ruby Red Cathedral Granite - S151G
3) Sky Blue/White Wispy Opalescent - S83391S
4) Dark Green/White Translucent Opalescent - S3276S
5) Dark Amber/White - S3176S
6) Medium Amber Smooth Cathedral- S1108SF
7) Opal White - S200S
8) Pale Grey Smooth Cathedral - S1808SF
9) Black Smooth Cathedral - S1009S
10) Yellow Smooth Cathedral - S161S

You will probably be able to use small sheets of everything but the Cherry Red & Sky Blue/White. For those two pieces of glass you will need either two small sheets (8x10) or one medium sheet (12x16) of glass. From here on the steps are the same as the last chapter right up to framing. The main thing is getting used to making difficult cuts. You may find that you need medium or even large sheets of glass for this project simply because you are having such difficulty making the cuts and thus need to recut pieces several times. Don't worry, that is what this project is all about - practicing you cutting technique.

And the only way to do that is to try making difficult cuts. The pattern is labeled "Light House" in the appendix.

Now is the time to introduce you to three products that could make your life a little easier. One is the Morton System Portable Glass Shop, another the Morton Safety Break System and the last is a Diamond Ring Saw. I don't recommend you use either product (except the Safety Break System) until you are able to make these kinds of cuts by hand. But once you have that skill, these products can save you a lot of time.

The Morton Portable Glass Shop sets up on either of the main brands of cutting surfaces but the Morton Maxi-Surface has pre-painted reference dots already on it to make set up easier. This product allows you to quickly and easily score difficult or repetitive shapes. It is great when you are going to have the exact same shaped piece or a lot of pieces of the same width. It is also good for repetitive designs like geometric lampshades or some types of modern art panels. The Safety Break System is three pieces of equipment that you can use to help you run a score line of any shape and length without having it break poorly. If you have a long score line and you try to use your running pliers the break often leaves the score line at a weak point in the glass. One way to fix this is to start the run on one end and then move to the other end and finish running it from the other side. But sometimes even this won't work. The Morton Safety Break System allows you to start a run and continue a run at any point along the score. It is a great tool for beginners and experts. It too works with either of the major cutting board systems and has a button you place under the score line where you want the run to start. Then you press down with one of two tools to start the break - elegantly simple yet so convenient.

The last item that you may wish to consider later on for difficult cuts is a diamond ring saw. These are different from diamond band saws. A ring saw is a ring of metal coated on all sides with diamonds. These are superior in my view to band saws because they allow you to cut in all directions and are also slightly safer as it is almost impossible to cut yourself on them. The best one on the market, though it can be a little pricey, is the Taurus III from Gemini, although there are other competing products that many people swear by. If you can afford it, and I did warn you that this was an expensive hobby, and you have already mastered difficult cuts, then this saw will enable you to speed up your production time considerably. That is really helpful around the holidays when you are trying as hard as you can to get 50 gifts done in time for the family gathering. It is also useful if you decide to make stained glass work into a side or main business as it eliminates the problem of bad breaks altogether.

Now back to the project at hand. There are several ways to frame an odd sized panel. The easiest is still to buy pre-fabricated sides, such as Pop-Lock, in the sizes needed. However, as you may notice, these only come in even numbers. Never fear, simply attach a zinc channel of sufficient width to the top and bottom of the piece to make it the required height. The channel will be completely hidden by the wood frame and you will have a beautifully framed panel. The other method you can use is the metal framing method described earlier.

Now let's move on to the free form window hanger. Look for the pattern labeled "Angel #1" in your appendix. Not only does this have difficult cuts and odd shapes but at the figure's head there is a halo that is attached to the head by a drop of solder. Plus, since this is an odd shape you will be unable to square off the piece and there are voids beneath the wings. Don't worry; all of these problems have solutions.

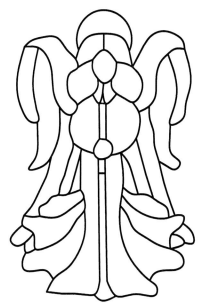

Start as always by making three copies of the pattern and label all of them. Now get ready to be introduced to a new type of glass. This is Armstrong Glass. Armstrong is another quality manufacturer of very smooth, easy to cut glass. They are especially renowned for their iridized glasses (shiny surfaced) that seem to reflect a rainbow on top of their actual color. Let's collect your glass.

You will need:

1) Armstrong Dark Green Cathedral - A33C
2) Armstrong Yellow Cathedral - 77S
3) Spectrum Black Smooth Cathedral - S1009S
4) Armstrong Medium Gray Opal Wispy - 111SO
5) Spectrum White Opal - S200S

Once again you should be able to make this pattern with one small sheet of each type of glass. Tack your layout pattern down using tacks at the four corners of your pattern. Now cut out all of your pieces as you have done before, grinding them smooth and foiling them. Lay them on their appropriate spots on your homasote board. Use tacks around the edge to hold the glass in place in relation to one another. Now the glass won't move and you'll be able to flux and solder properly. Tinning also provides a special problem. Whenever an object has voids within it, as between the wings and the body, either prop the piece up or have one hand wearing a heavy leather glove to allow you access to the holes. In this way you can tin the foil while still leaving the void. You should never attempt to float a void of this size.

As for the halo, simply lay the piece backside facing up. First tin the entire halo. You can either purchase a premade metal halo, or make your own using tinned wire. Find the spot where you'd like the halo to stay. Then hold the soldering iron on any points where the halo overlaps a solder seam. It might help to have that leather gloved hand or a pair of pliers holding the overhanging part of the halo steady during this process. Once the halo is tack soldered in this manner, build up a small bead of solder over the points where the halo crosses the solder line.

Oddly shaped projects pose a unique challenge when it comes to reinforcement. The best way is to get either u-channel lead came, copper covered steel strips, or pre-tinned wire. If you are using wire, simply use the same procedure described in the suncatcher lesson. However, this will be inadequate reinforcement for larger free-form objects. You can buy steel ribbon coated in copper to use as reinforcement as well. We will discuss another use for this product in a later chapter. But for these purposes you would wrap it around the piece just like the wire and solder it in place. The only difficulty is in dealing with its rigidity. It will not like being bent and held in place. The final method is also the best looking. Get suncatcher sized u-channel lead came and, after stretching it as described in the lead came lesson later in this book, wrap it around the piece. It will be easy to wrap, although you may have some problems at inside corners. Never fear just cut the came at angles and fit them together like a mitered joint. Solder any joints together and tin the entire lead came. Now you have a beautifully edged piece that will accept patina and have an even edge all the way around.

You are now ready to tackle these projects:

1) Any Spectrum Pattern of the Month found in the program Glass Eye 2000
2) Firefighter Cluster
3) Beveled Cross

LESSON 7 - INTRODUCTION TO THREE DIMENSIONAL OBJECTS

Okay, you are now ready for the big leagues. It's time to make your first 3-D object, a business card holder. You'll need all the tools we've used before plus these new supplies and tools that are essential. You have to, at this point, buy a set of Wedgie Jrs. It is just not possible to use any other tool to adequately make three-dimensional objects. There are others on the market, but none that I have found to be satisfactory. They come in sets of three. I recommend buying two sets so that you have six total. They are made of heat and chemical resistant foam and are a must. The other things you will need for this project are bevels & pre-cast metal feet. I like using closed right-angle feet. But you can choose lead ball & claw feet, ball feet or any type of foot, as long as it is metal. A bevel is a piece of glass that has had the edges cut at a 15-degree angle to create wonderful light refractions. For this project you will need two 1x4 inch bevels (or one bevel and one piece of glass for the bottom and of the same dimensions), two 1x1 inch bevels and one 2x4 inch bevel. I suggest ordering colored bevels. I've always found pale blue or green to work well with this project.

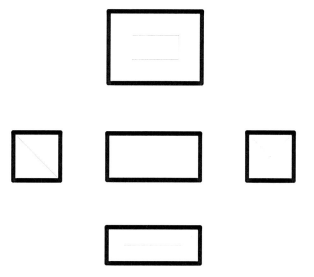

You start by foiling your pieces as you always would. In this case I suggest
using silver backed tape as the final product will look nice with silver seams.
Don't worry about the feet being brass colored that can be changed. Once
you have foiled all the pieces, use the wedgies to help you form a right angle
between a 1x4 & a 1x1 piece. Be sure they are both stabilized so they won't
move. Now dab flux along the edges. Press through with solder to hold the
pieces in place. You will want to use flat seams on the outside of your object
so don't put too much solder on. Now flip the piece over and using wedgies
to stabilize it, solder the inside after applying flux. Now get the other 1x1 and
solder it to the other side of the 1x4. Be creative with the wedgies for your
stabilization. Once you've soldered inside and out, solder the 2x4 piece in
place making sure that this creates a flat bottom and that the extra part of the
2x4 is sticking out at one side. Place the last 1x4 down on the work surface.
Lay the box on top of it and point solder on the inside to hold it in place. Flip
the piece over and use wedgies to level it out. Flat solder along the seams.
Turn it right side up again and finish soldering the inside. Now tin around the
edges.

Congratulations, you've just made a 3-D object. That wasn't so bad, was it? Well you're not done yet. Flip the piece back over and stabilize with wedgies. Holding a foot with a pair of pliers or a gloved hand, heat the solder around the projecting prongs. This will lightly tack the foot in place. Once tacked, add more solder on the inside angle of the foot and cardholder to stabilize. Do this four times. To tin the feet and make them the same color as the seams, coat the feet with flux and then lightly add solder to the foot. The solder will cover the foot evenly and match the rest of the piece. Now just clean the whole thing off with you flux cleaner and polish it up with your finishing compound. Now your fancy business card holder is truly completed and you can show off your handiwork at the office.

Now that you've made a cardholder with pre-cut pieces, let's make a small jewelry box out of plain glass. Look for the pattern "Jewelry Box #1" in the appendix. It is a simple piece made up of only six pieces. However, you will be working with a new type of glass, Youghiogheny glass, that can be difficult to break and is sometimes of uneven thickness but that comes in such splendid colors that it is worth it. You will also be making a hinge for the first time. Another way to do this is to use precut bevels for the sides and top, and a beveled mirror for the bottom.

Supplies: Youghiogheny Lavender, Gold & Pink Y-3007RG Glass, 24-gauge wire, 30-gauge brass tube, 4 brass ball feet, all basic glass supplies.

First copy, label & cut out two patterns. Since each side is a single piece of glass you don't need a layout copy. Foil & solder the bottom and sides together just like you did for the business card holder. Now stick the wire through the tube. You have to put in at least 3.5 inches of wire into the tube. Now cut a 3-inch length of tube. The wire prevented the tube from crushing in on itself. Discard the unused piece of wire left in the unused tubing. Shove more wire through so that you have an inch of wire sticking out each end of the tube. Next, solder the tube to the lid of the box and tin the edges. Now comes the tricky part. Bend the wire, sticking out of each end, so that it has a 90 degree angle bend at each end. Solder the wire ends to the seams between the sides and the back of the main box. For an added flourish you can create a loop of wire as we've talked about before and solder that to the middle of the front of the lid to act as an opener. Now solder on the feet as before. You can also solder a short length of fine chain between the lid and one side. This keeps the lid from opening past a certain point. If the chain is short enough that the lid cannot be raised to vertical, then it will also act as an automatic closer for the box.

You are now ready to tackle:

1) 3-D Art Deco Card Holder
2) Dove Box
3) Celtic Cross Box
4) Simple Bevel Card Holder
5) Cross Card Holder

LESSON 8 - DECORATIVE SOLDERING

There will be times, for example when you are making a box or special gift that you want to add a nice decorative flourish. That's where decorative soldering comes into play. Believe it or not you've already learned one decorative technique - soldering on feet to a box. But there is plenty more for you to learn. To get ready for your decorative soldering session you will need to get six strips of glass 1 inch wide by 7 inches long and flat solder them together so that you have a working board 6 inches by 7 inches. It doesn't matter what type of glass just make sure you don't put beads on any of the seams. You will also need the following tools:

Tools & Supplies: Wire Twister or Pre-Twisted Wire, Copper Sheet, Glass Nuggets, Sponge.

In case you are wondering, a wire twister is a great little device that quickly and easily twists wire or lead came into a spiral for decorative use. It is great because it means you don't have to buy pre-twisted wire and can instead just use your existing supply of wire when you want to decorate. This can be a significant cost savings over time. Plus, you can wind together wires of two different widths for some very interesting effects.

Decorative Technique #1 - Sponging

This is by far my favorite technique and also one of the easiest to apply. Simply choose a section of seam (an inch or two will do) for this, flux it and add a very high bead to it. While the bead is still hot, touch it with a wet sponge. Dab the sponge all up and down the seam. Notice how it creates this create mottled appearance, almost like metal nuggets. When combined with other techniques, this can give a startlingly organic feel to your soldering.

Decorative Technique #2 - Droplets

Droplets are a fun way to add interest to a border. Go to a section of seam that still has a flat solder line. Flux it. Now, press through the solder to create a small circular bead on the seam. Move along the seam and press down a second one just far enough away so that the two beads don't touch. Continue doing this for five or six droplets. Notice how you can create a wonderful scalloped appearance.

To add dramatic effect use a Wedgie Jr. to hold the working surface at an angle. Now do the same thing except this time gravity will pull down on the bead slightly forming teardrop shapes. If you do the teardrops or the beads really close together the scalloping is tighter and it can even overlap for the teardrop technique (though this looks far too much like a set of double chins for my taste).

Decorative Technique #3 - Drawing Solder

This technique requires a section of bead and glass with absolutely no flux at all. Add a high bead to a seam and then use the corner of your soldering iron to pull some solder onto the glass. It should look like a thorn. For dramatic effect you can do a series of thorns or to create the look of a thorned stem for a flower. You can also continue this thorn by pressing down through solder at the end of the thorn. You can keep doing this until you have created a bridge from one seam to another. You can even create a series of bridges. Practice this because you'll need two bridges only about an inch apart from each other for the next technique.

Decorative Technique #4 - Attaching Nuggets/Jewels

Nuggets are small rounded beads of glass that have one flat side. Jewels are similar except they have actual facets on them. Some artists use jewel to refer to both smooth and faceted varieties. There are two ways you can attach a nugget/jewel to your piece. One way is actually cheating in my book. Simply apply a drop of super-glue to the back of your nugget and then attach it to the glass. However, since there is nothing apparently holding the nugget in place this can look unnatural. My preferred method is as follows. Place your nugget in a corner between two bridges of solder. Try to position it so that there is one edge of the nugget on a seam and other edges on each bridge. Now press through solder around the base of the nugget and build up along the sides.

This can be made even more interesting by creating a wire holder for the nugget and propping it up then covering the wire frame entirely with solder. It will look like the nugget is on a mountain, especially if you combine this with the sponging technique. Also, you can combine a series of nuggets together for a naturalistic look.

Decorative Technique #5 - Attaching Wire

Attaching a twisted wire or plain wire to a piece is an easy way to add a decorative flourish. Say you have a butterfly on a panel or suncatcher. Instead of using glass for the antenna you can take your wire, twist one end around a pencil a few times to get the rounded end and then leave a portion strait. Cut the wire and solder the free end to the head of the butterfly. Do this twice and you have a set of antennae. You can also use twisted wire to create special effects, such as mullions on windows within a panel scene or stems for flowers. Wire can also be used to create an interesting border around suncatchers and lamps. One easy way is to create a very long length of twisted wire and bend it into a series of scallops. Then solder the bottom part of each scallop to the base of your lamp. Now you have a decorative trim that is truly unique. Decorative wire can also be used in other ways. On this jewelry box it is used as a handle. You've already done this once before when you gave the Angel a halo!

Decorative Technique #6 - Drawing & Molding Solder Shapes

Take that flat piece of copper sheet and using the press through technique to draw a shape onto the sheet. When you are finished let it cool. After it cools you can just bend the sheet and peel off the shape. Once peeled you can solder it flat onto your glass or just solder an edge and have it sticking out in a 3-D shape. This is a great way to create insect wings. You can also create little scenes or shapes to apply using glue to your framing. Another way to create shapes with solder is to buy clay molds and fill them with solder. Once the solder dries you can tap the clay on the table and the shape will fall out. You can solder these shapes directly onto other seams. Just be careful. The shapes are made of solder and will melt out of shape if you heat them too long.

Decorative Soldering Technique #7 - Filigree

Filigree is simply a piece of metal that has been cut into a particular shape (an angel's halo or a dragon fly's wing) and then had sections of it punched out to make it see through. The best way to work with filigree is to cut a piece of glass to the exact size of the filigree. Assemble your pattern as you normally would. Then tin the filigree in the same manner that you would tin a wire or the edge of a panel. Place the filigree on top of the desired piece and then heat the edges. It will melt into the solder bead at the seam. For added support you can also add more solder to smooth the edges.

Another way to use filigree is to still tin the filigree, so it will accept the same patina as the rest of the piece, but attach it only at one point so that the rest of it sticks out as a three dimensional object. This is an especially interesting effect with angel halos.

LESSON 9 - LAMPS & FIXTURES

The easiest lamp to make by far is the Fan Lamp. This involves a wooden or metal base with the lamp hardware and a slot to hold a fan shaped panel of glass upright in front of the light. It is the easiest of the lamps because you are not required to make a three-dimensional component. Instead you simply make a fan shaped panel and make sure that the section that goes in the slot has been flat soldered and the rest has good beading.

To do this you will need your standard supplies as well as a fan lamp base. You can buy the base at a stained glass supply store or online. For this fan

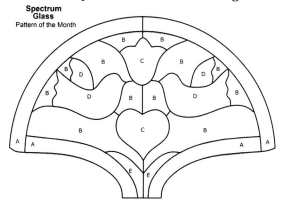

lamp we will be making one of the Spectrum Glass Patterns of the Month that was designed by Paul Harman. It is listed in the appendix as "Spectrum Pattern of the Month: Country Fan."

You will need the following Spectrum Glasses:

1) White/Yellow Semi-Translucent Opalescent - S3651S
2) White/Clear Semi-Translucent Opalescent - S305S
3) Red/White Wispy Opalescent - S-3591S
4) Dark Blue/White Translucent Opalescent - S-3376S
5) Dark Green/White Wispy Opalescent - S-3296S

Once again, you can order these by number online or through your local stained glass supply store. One of the nicest things about the fan lamp is that since the fan simply sits inside a slot on the base you can replace it easily and completely change the décor of the room in which it resides. This makes fan lamps one of the most versatile decorating tools. It also means that you can buy one fan base and make an unlimited number of fan shapes to fit your mood. Plus, fans are fun to make.

Since the fan is not a regular shape you can't square it off using the Morton layout blocks in the traditional fashion. However, it is critical that the bottom be flat and the sides symmetrical for the fan lamp to work properly. If the bottom is not perfectly flat or if the fan is lop-sided then it will fall out of its base. Remember, there is only about 1 1/2 inches of glass inserted into the slot at the bottom but the fan itself is about 10 inches wide. The slightest imbalance could tip it over. That is why you still need to use the Morton blocks, just in an innovative fashion.

Use your first block to provide a stable and flat support for the base. Now take two short pieces and place them supporting the corners of the fan at an angle. Finally, put a block at the top of the piece. Once your pieces are all cut out you will use tacks along the outer edge like when you worked on the free-form window hanger to hold the other pieces in place. The rest goes just like a simple panel would.

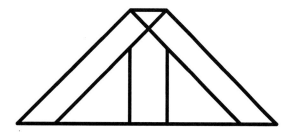

Now things get a little harder. For the flat panel lamp, you will combine the skills you used to make a hanging panel with the skills of three-dimensional objects to make a flat panel shade that can be used on a lamp or on a pendant style hanging light fixture. Find the design marked "Light Fixture" in the appendix. The design itself is quite simple. However you will need six copies of this pattern, one for your layout pattern, four for the four sides of the lamp, plus a spare. You will also need a 1 inch wide square vase cap. This will be what the top of each section is soldered to and what will hold the lamp to the overhead fixture or lamp base, depending on your needs. If you are making a lampshade it is best to get a vented cap so that heat can escape. This is not an issue with overhead fixtures. Either way you will need to enlarge the pattern so that the short side fits into the vase cap. Also, the large rectangle at the top of the pattern is designed to be soldered at an angle to the lampshade but at right angles to the other rectangles on the other sides.

When you are squaring off the panel be careful so that the top, shortest side, has only one small Morton block or none at all. That way as you tack solder each section you can simply remove the top block and pry up the panel leaving the other blocks in place. This way each panel will be squared to exactly the same shape.

First make each of the four sections just as you have learned before. Now take each of the finished sides and lean them up against each other. Use masking tape at the top and bottom corners to hold them in place. Run a strip of masking tape down each seam. Now turn the piece over and solder the inside seams while your shade is supported by your Wedgie Jrs. The piece of masking tape will help you float any voids along the seam. When you are done flip the piece over and remove the masking tape. Now flat solder the outside seams. Once the sides are all soldered to each other, flip it over once more and rest the top inside the vase cap. Use your Wedgie Jrs. to help hold it in place. Now solder the top edge to the vase cap.

Tiffany Style Lamps are by far the most complex of lamps. Not only do they usually involve much smaller pieces than other lampshade styles but they also are built up on sloping or curved molds instead of using flat working surfaces. They are such complex objects that the beginner should not even attempt them. Practice the other forms and once you feel ready check out my upcoming advanced techniques book for instructions on working on and designing Tiffany Style Lamps.

You are now ready to try:

1) Patriotic Lamp
2) Rainbow Lamp

LESSON 10 - CLOCKS

One of the most requested items from your friends and family when they learn of your newfound skill will be for stained glass clocks. Clocks can take many different shapes and sizes. In this lesson we will discuss three: pedestal, framed & framed pendulum. Each has its own unique sets of problems and issues that must be solved.

The first type of clock we will approach is the pedestal clock. Now all clock projects come in kits. Or I should say, the clockwork parts come in kits. There aren't many people I know out there who could create their own clockworks, gears and all. With pedestal clocks the clockworks usually come along with the pedestal base as well as a pattern for a suggested look. We will be working with one of those kits for the pedestal clock in this book. From a stained glass dealer, purchase Clockworks Kit that has either just the insertable clock or the clock and base. If you your kit does not come with a base you will need to purchase one separately or make one yourself.

Find a pedestal clock kit with a pattern like from either an online merchant or your local stained glass shop. I also suggest that you order, if you haven't already, a Spectrum glass value box of some sort so that you will have a wide variety of glass to choose from for this project. Choose the glass from the box that fits the colors you would like for the clock. Now, take the pattern that comes with your clock and make three copies. Remember what I said earlier about copier enlargements? Well, the pedestal on this project is designed with slots that assume that there will be a slight increase in size from the printed pattern. So if you don't photocopy it then the size will be all wrong.

The big challenge on this clock is getting everything to fit together properly before soldering. There will be a large hole in the upper portion for the clock to fit into and the arched sides do not lend themselves to the Morton layout system. Use the layout blocks for the three straight sides and just tack the other two pieces in place. This procedure will be similar to the tacking you did for a free-form hanging object like Angel #1. Now flux and tack solder as usual. Be sure that all of your seams are flat soldered at first. We'll go back later on and add beads.

Once you have soldered the front of the piece slip the metal clock holder through the hole so that the brass lip is touching the tinned edges of the whole. Solder the back of the piece using full beads except on the parts that will slide into the groove on the pedestal and put a nice circle of solder around the clock holder. Now flip the piece over. It will actually be resting on the metal clockworks holder now. Add full beads to the front seams everywhere except where the glass will be in the pedestal groove. Now clean off all the flux and patina as before. Once you slide the clockworks into its holder and the panel into the groove your clock is finished (except for buying a battery for it of course).

Other clocks are handled in a similar manner except extra care is needed if it is a pendulum clock. Be sure that space is provided for the swinging motion. A framed clock or framed pendulum clock can be the most challenging. This is because not only must you build a glass item that will have moving parts inserted but usually these come in kits with a pre-made frame. That means that you must be absolutely sure that your pieces fit together perfectly so that your glass doesn't distort into any shape other than that of the frame or grow past the edges of the frame. This is not a problem when the frame is made after the fact but is a problem when the frame is made ahead of time.

LESSON 11 - LEAD CAME WORK

Up until now all of your work has been with the copper foil technique of stained glass production. Now we'll move on to the older and messier technique of using lead came (pronounced cām). Lead came is a strip of lead that has been molded along its entire length (it usually sells in 6 foot lengths or in a roll) into either a U or H channel. In addition the flanges can be either rounded or flat. It also comes in different widths, from thin "suncatcher" width to massive 1/2 inch wide flanges. Each has its uses.

Either way, after the glass fits into the channel, the part that shows is the flange, and the center bar of an H channel/back of a U channel is the heart. When you are dealing with lead came you will need some special tools that you didn't need for copper foil. One tool that you will still use is your fid/lathkin.

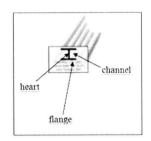

Some other tools are:

1) **Lead Cutter/Dykes** - This nifty little tool cuts your lead came. One of the blade sides is straight and that's the side you keep towards the section you want to work with. The other has an angle and that goes towards the unused section since you usually want flat ends on your lead. Obviously

that means that you'll have to flip your cutters over to knip off the angled bit when you're ready to cut off more lead. This can lead to waste, but many people prefer the cutters for ease of use. Always cut parallel to the heart of the came otherwise you will crush the sides.

2) **Lead Knife** - This is my preferred method of cutting came. It is a knife that rocks across the lead and gives you a straight cut on both sides. No waste with this tool. But it is a knife and some people have problems or are scared of using it.

3) **Lead Stretcher** - When you buy lead it will be straight at your supply store but the minute you pull it out of the crate it'll bend. Or it might have gotten bumped or slumped in the box during shipping. If you really like lead came work you buy it on a roll because it is more economical that way. Either way you need to stretch the lead before use. This takes all the kinks out of the lead and also lengthens it slightly. Your lead will be stronger, less likely to sag over time and hold your glass better if it is properly stretched. Lead stretchers come in two varieties. The first is a simple vise that installs on a table. You put one end of the lead in the vise; you grab the other with a pair of pliers; then you pull on it as hard as you can for a short while. The second is a machine that automates this process and keeps you from falling backwards onto your behind when either the lead gives way or your grip on the pliers slips.

4) **Working Board** - When you worked on copper foil you used homasote as your working board. Now it would be better to have a plywood table or a large piece of plywood as your surface. I find that a big 24x24x1/2 inch plywood square is best. Plus you can buy it precut to that size in most home improvement stores. You will then need to nail strips of wood along two sides forming a right angle. Make sure it is a right angle.

5) **Horseshoe Nails** - With copper foil the pieces just sat on the paper until you tack soldered them in place. With lead came you need to hold them inside the channel while you get the next piece ready. To do this you hammer nails into the plywood just enough to hold things in place.

6) **Li'l Notcher** - Every piece of lead work is framed out in metal as it is being built. You will use the same metal channel that you used for framing your copper foil work. The Li'l Notcher cuts out 90 degree notches in the 1/8" channel making your framing job much easier. If you decide to use 1/8" came for framing your copper foil work this is an easy way to do the corners. Just notch out the corners and bend the came around your piece. It also comes in a 45 degree model.

7) **Brass Brush** - After you have soldered the lead came together the joints will sometimes oxidize. You use the brass brush to rub the white oxidation off.

8) **Lead Came Putty/Mud/Black Cement** - This is a black mud-like substance that you rub into the joints between glass and lead came after the piece is all soldered together. The purpose of this is to fill the gaps, make the panel watertight and act as a shock absorber for the glass. This is why lead came work is preferred over copper foil in situations where the piece is likely to be jarred frequently, such as a front door.

9) **Mudding Brush** - This is a simple small brush that you use to force the mud into the seams. A second brush is used to rub whiting over it and burnish the lead. This gives the lead the traditional black look. The more a brush is used the better the look.

10) **Whiting** - This is essentially chalk powder. After you have finished mudding, you cover the piece with whiting and rub it with the other brush. This will absorb excess mud and finish your product.

11) **Lead Pattern Cutting Shears** - Almost forgot these. These are just like the foil pattern cutting shears except they take a bigger bite out of the paper to accommodate the larger heart of lead came.

Okay, now that you've gotten yet another shopping list, let's get on with our project. Hopefully you like quilts, because this project is a quilt square - It's a little known fact that quilt patterns are perfect for conversion into stained glass patterns and vice-versa. You'll also be using bevels in this project. Bevels are pre-cut pieces that have angled sides. They give a jeweled or faceted feel and can come in either clear, colors or glue-chip. In this case you'll be using clear diamond bevels. Bevels can be fun to work with but make sure that your pattern is scaled properly so that your bevels will fit correctly. This may take some trial and error at the copy machine so take your bevels with you to Kinko's.

This project is called "Quilting Star" in your Appendix. You'll only have to cut 12 pieces of glass and each cut is fairly simple. You'll also need to buy four bevels and the bevels will determine the size of your pattern. Or, if you don't want to bother just substitute clear glass of the same shape. For this piece we'll let you choose the other two colors. I'm using a Pink and White combination but just choose something from your own collection of glass that you like. It's time to strut your stuff.

Your next choice is what size channel you will use for framing your work. Take a small snippet of that channel and place it so that the heart of the channel lies on the edge of the pattern. Mark with a line the flange overlap onto the glass and the framing that sticks out past the pattern. Continue these lines all the way around your pattern. Cut out two of the zinc framing pieces to their appropriate sizes and place them in the squared off corner of the work surface. Now place one copy of your pattern onto your working surface so that the outside edge of the framing is lined up with the flange overlap line you drew on your pattern. This will ensure a nice tight square fit.

Next cut out all your glass and lay them out on the pattern. Ensure that they fit loosely together and grind as necessary. Then start by placing only one piece at a time into the channel of the frame. (I'd start with piece #8 on the picture). Cut lead came to the length of each side and then move onto the next piece. As you are moving on you will be hammering and then removing the horseshoe nails to hold pieces in place. If you want to keep from damaging glass that doesn't have lead in place yet, use a little piece of scrap came to act as a buffer between nail & glass. Continue this process until you are all the way around. Now, on the two sides abutting the already cut framing, cutting the lead so that it butts up against the frame is easy. You just place the lead beside the piece, mark it and cut it. On the other two sides, without metal framing yet, it can be more difficult. Make your cut mark where the inner line is that you drew on your pattern earlier. This way the lead will have a nice flush joint with the zinc frame later. If you are using lead nippers, have the flat side of the nippers facing towards the part of the lead you plan to keep for those joints that are T-junctions (90° angles) and have the beveled side facing the lead you plan to keep for those junctions where the lead meets at anything other than a 90° angle. By doing this you will have much neater and cleaner looking joints for a more professional appearance. If you are using a lead knife you have the ability to create the exact angle you need. Just make certain that you place the lead on the table on its side so that as you rock the knife back and forth you do not crush the channel closed.

Once all your glass and lead is in place along with the other two sides of zinc the only thing holding it all together will still be pressure from the nails on the backside of the zinc channel. Flux the corners of the frame and also the points where the lead butts up against the frame. Use your soldering iron to preheat the zinc. Be careful to only preheat the zinc. It is possible to completely melt your lead came at this stage. Zinc is a heat sink and if you try to just solder directly onto it you'll melt your lead before the zinc has properly heated. After you've preheated the zinc then apply 60/40 solder to the joint. Just press through and lift. Continue all the way around the piece edge. Now flux the individual lead joints and solder each of those with the light press through method. Don't hold down for any length of time or the lead came will melt. Be extra careful not to touch the soldering iron directly onto the lead came. Don't remove the nails and prepare to move on until you are absolutely sure that you have soldered EVERY SINGLE JOINT! I must emphasize this point. Make sure every joint is soldered before moving on.

Once you are sure, take out the nails flip the piece over and repeat the process on the back.

Guess what comes next? That's right. After you are positive that all joints are soldered, then clean off the flux. Next, use your mud brush to press the mud into the joints. Use a brushing motion where you push down and in so that you really press it into place. You can also use your hands but a brush is neater. After you have finished one side flip it over. If you did a good job mudding the first side, then any loose joints between glass and lead will have mud oozing through them onto the other side. Now mud the second side with the same method.

Once the mud is in place either throw away the brush or put it inside several Ziploc bags (one inside the other) and put it in the freezer. If you let it sit out it will stink up the place, harden and be unusable. If you don't keep it protected from the food in the freezer it will impart a funny smell and taste to anything else in the freezer.

Now it's time for whiting. Sprinkle lots of whiting on the piece and then have at it with another brush. Just keep scrubbing in circles until you have cleaned all the mud off the glass but not so hard that you take any out of the seams. When the glass is clean, flip it over and do the other side. Keep this brush and always and only use it for this step. As you do more work it will get blacker and blacker and impart a nicer and nicer patina to the lead lines. This is the step that turns those silver solder marks and grey lead lines to black.

You're not done yet. Let the piece sit for at least two days. During this time some of the mud will ooze out of the seams. Don't apply any more whiting but do brush it again on both sides.

Now, you might be done. Unless you framed with brass channel instead of zinc and want your joints and seams golden/brassy. You can even use bendable brass-capped lead for the internal lines. This is very popular for decorative door inserts. If you did this, then you will need to paint all of the joints. To get that nice gold look, get out a paint pen and color them gold. You could also take the metal framing and slip it inside a specially designed wooden frame, such as the Pop-Lock system, so that your lead work is framed out in wood.

Now, for door inserts some people like even the frame to be in lead came. This lets them fit it more precisely since they can slice off parts of the lead where it doesn't quite fit the door. The choice is up to you. H-channel lead framing make fitting into architectural openings easier, but hard metal framing - such as brass or zinc - provides greater structural support and rigidity. By now you should be mastering techniques and learning more and more about what can and cannot be done with glass.

You can take any square or rectangular panel pattern and use the lead came method to create it. Once you are advanced enough you can even use a special tool known as a came bender to create round or oval frames for use with lead came.

LESSON 12 - DESIGNING YOUR OWN PATTERNS

There comes a time in every glass hobbyist's life when they grow tired of slavishly copying from pattern books and want to draw their own patterns. Basically you could just take pen, paper, sketch it out, and make copies; but that's not the best way. Drafting tools make things even easier, as does oversized paper (you can use those great big pads that are often used in the boring staff meetings you hate). But the best way is with a computer program. Here is where I do another unpaid product endorsement. If you want the best program for ease of use, then check out Glass Eye 2000 from Dragonfly Software (*www.dfly.com*). It has a great tutorial that will have you designing in no time. It also contains a large number of easy to create "Spectrum Patterns of the Month" which I highly recommend you use for practice. These patterns can also be downloaded from the Spectrum web site (*www.spectrumglass.com*). A trial version of the program is included on the CD version of this book or for download via a special web address provided at the end of this book.

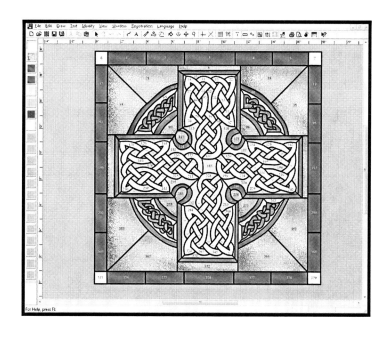

This program has all sorts of patterns included in case you find yourself in a creative slump. But it makes designing a breeze. Plus, as you choose colors the program helps you find the exact glass that will give you that effect and then gives you the manufacturer and stock number for the glass. It even knows what kinds of bevels are out there for people. And it has another neat function. You can take a picture or other graphic, import it into the background and then draw your lines and place glass over the top so that you can make a stained glass design out of just about anything, even that old picture of grandma in the hallway. Or you can have the program trace the pattern for you! Finally it can print out the patterns onto multiple pages for oversized patterns. Then all you have to do is tape it together for a final copy.

This is the program that I have used throughout this book to design the example patterns and also the program used to design all the patterns in the appendix. I highly recommend it.

As for design, there are a couple of things to keep in mind. If you have no graphic design experience, try to keep color in mind. Too many colors in one piece can be over powering. Also keep cutting in mind. How easy will it be to cut the piece you just drew? Is it even possible to cut the piece you just drew? At this point you might want to go get a basic book on graphic design or color theory. Of course the easiest way is just to experiment. Take one of the existing patterns and modify it. Or if you are making a pattern off a picture, just match all the colors in the picture.

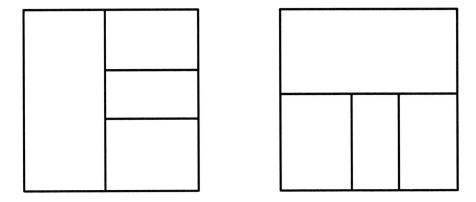

Balance is something people often fail to take into consideration. Look at the two pictures above this paragraph. It has one large piece of glass along one side and several smaller pieces of glass on the other. Not only does the glass look uneven but it has a major weak point. The entire piece could bend along the centerline and break. If you were to rotate the piece, as shown beside the first image, and put the solid piece on top, its weight would naturally cause the entire piece to bend along the middle line and break. Never arrange your pieces so that there is ever one continuous line all the way across a piece and never leave a piece so unbalanced that it has a natural bending point. Using the same amount of glass but breaking up the pieces will make for a more pleasing design and will lead to a longer lasting work of art.

When you are designing your pieces you may one day get very daring and create pieces larger in any given dimension than about 30 inches. At this point you will need to start adding reinforcement. If you are working in lead came you can buy steel rebar at your supply store or online supplier and then simply bend it to fit the shape of one of your lead lines. Then just solder it along the back. It will protrude slightly but since it is on the back no one will notice. If you are working in copper foil, use the tinned steel ribbon I mentioned earlier and simply place an appropriate length in between the pieces of copper foil. This will reinforce the piece. You can also insert tinned steel ribbon into the channel of your lead came, between the heart and the glass, to act as reinforcement - threading it from the frame on one side all the way to the other prior to soldering.

You may find that for extremely large pieces you need to reinforce in multiple locations. This is something you will learn intuitively over time. One last note on reinforcement; always reinforce perpendicular to the long dimension. This may seem counter-intuitive but that is the traditional method of reinforcing and it works well. If your window is the figure on the left, then reinforce it as shown on the right. Of course, your reinforcement lines don't have to be straight lines; they can be curved to fit the shape of your pattern. What is important is that they are perpendicular to the long side of the pattern.

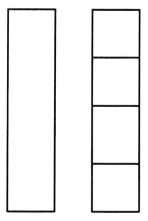

Finally, don't be too critical of yourself. What you make will be always beautiful, even if only to you. Now go out there and make some glass projects.

APPENDIX 1 - PROJECT PATTERNS & MORE

This appendix contains the full page patterns for all projects included in the chapters as well as several more you might want to tackle. Remember, don't be afraid. Just do it.

Southwest Deco Suncatcher

(use at current size)

Fly the Flag

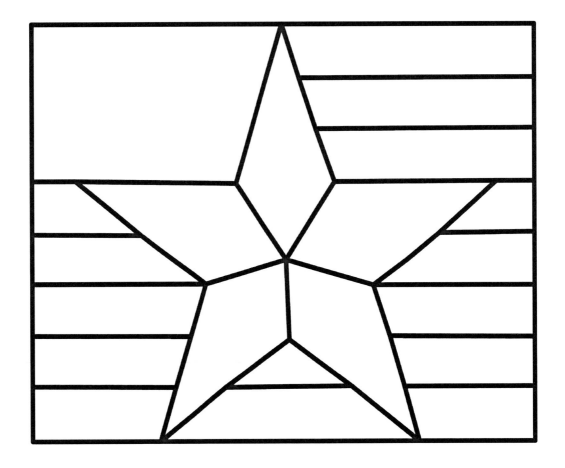

(enlarge to 8 x 10 size)

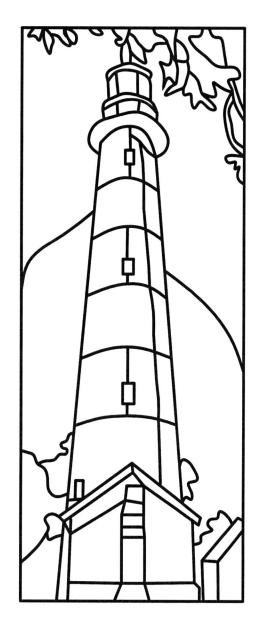

(enlarge to 6 x 12 or greater)

Angel #1

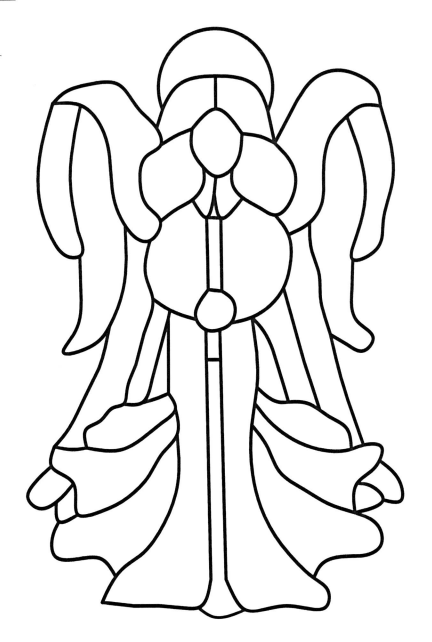

Simple Box

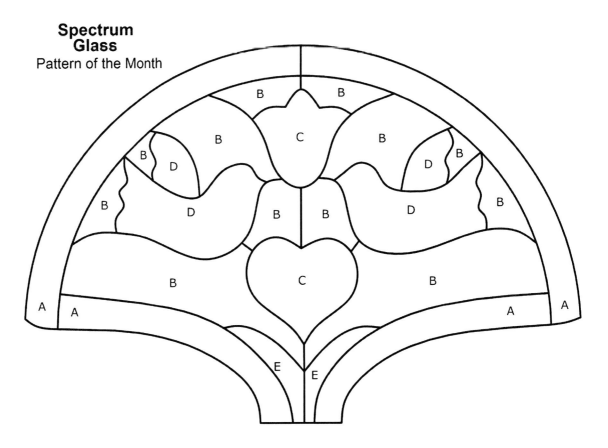

(enlarge to 9.5 x 6.25)

Light Fixture

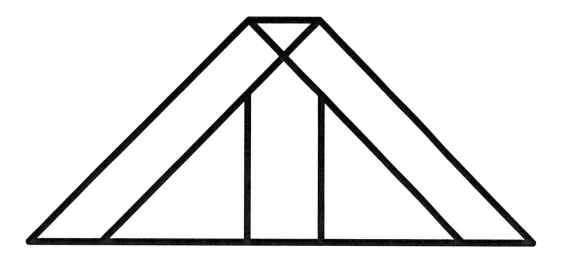

(expand so that short side of pattern fits into vase cape)

Quilting Star

(use at current size or alter to fit bevels)

Caduceus

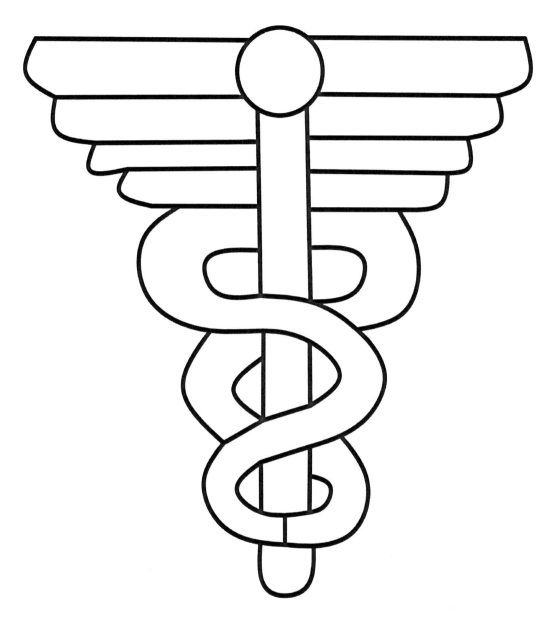

(enlarge as desired)

Easy Shamrock

(enlarge as desired)

Firefighter Suncatcher

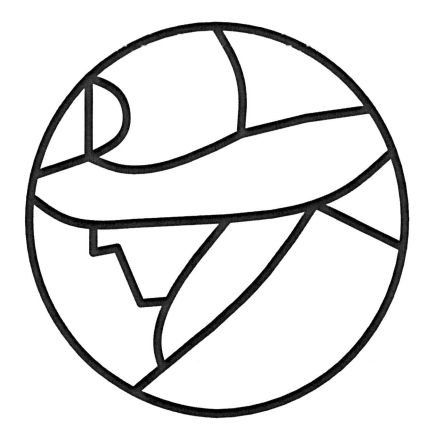

(repeat for larger quilts)

Welcome Sign

Personalize with House # or Name on Rectangle
using Hobby Glass Paint available at most hobby stores

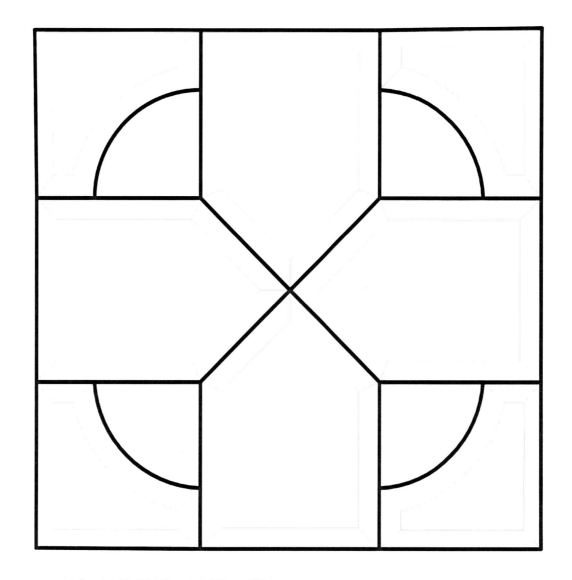

(Decorations on cross should be done using decorative solder)

3-d Art Deco Card Holder #1

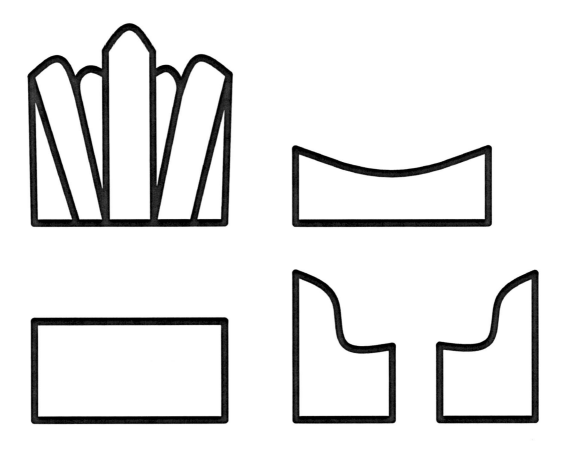

(Enlarge until front and back are larger than a business card)

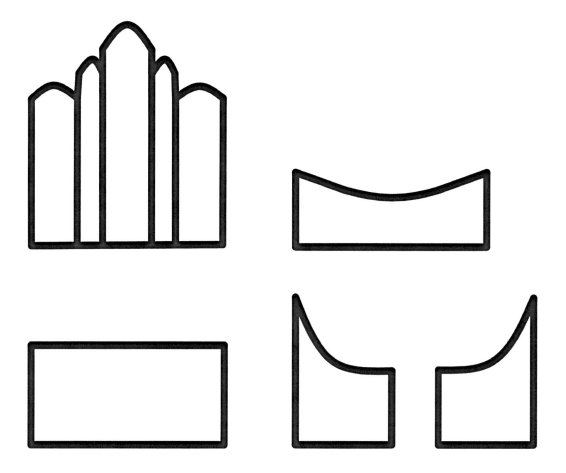

(Enlarge until front and back are larger than a business card)

Bevel Card Holder

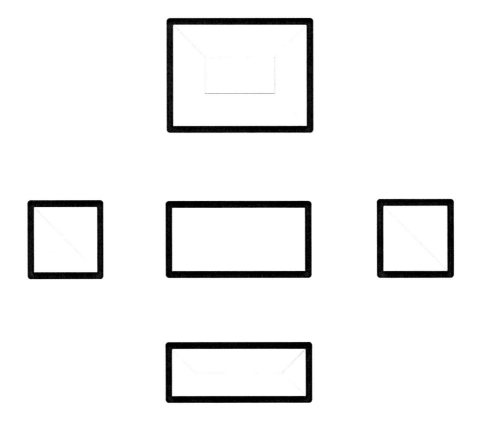

(Enlarge until front bevel is 1x4)

Cross Card Holder

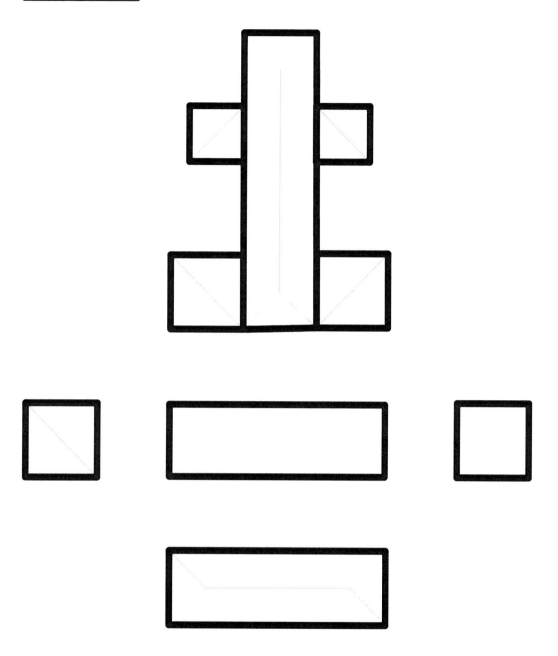

(Stabilize edge of cross and top of card holder with brass or zinc 1/8" U channel)
(Enlarge until front bevel is 1x4)

Dove Box

top   bottom

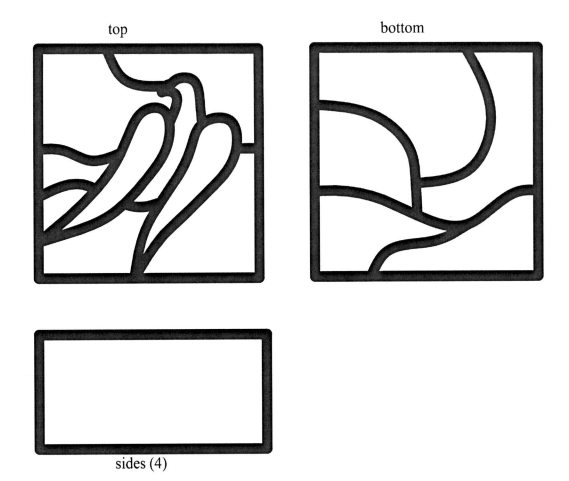

sides (4)

(Attach brass feet and use tube hinge on one side of top)
(Enlarge as desired)

Celtic Cross Box

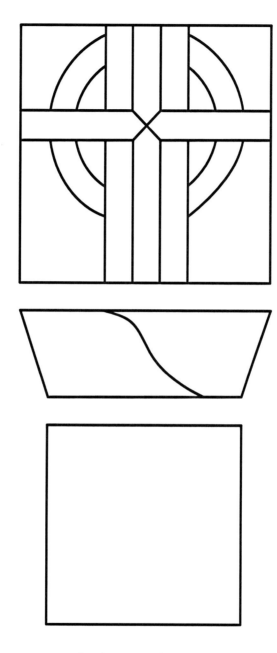

(Enlarge as desired)

(Box bevels down at bottom to a smaller sized base)

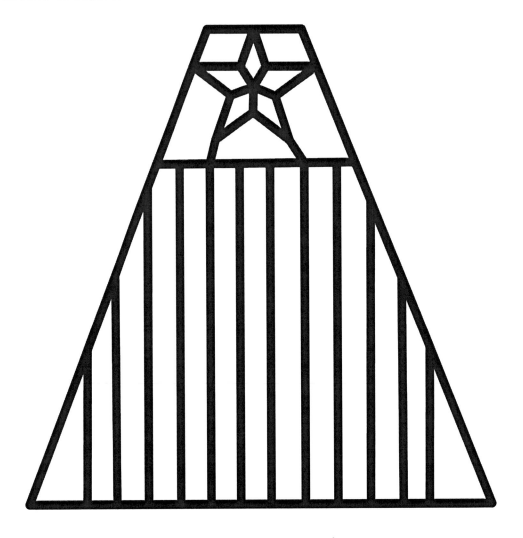

(Enlarge to fit vase cap)

Rainbow Shade

(Enlarge so short end fits into vase cap, bottom rectangle designed to be
soldered at angle to main lamp shade section)

9-11 - In Memoriam

This is my special tribute to my fallen firefighter brothers
who fell in the line of duty on 9-11-01.

(Enlarge to 28 x 20)

copyright 2002 Phillip C. McKee, III

All Rights Reserved.

Three Memories of Loss on 9-11

My tribute to all those who died that horrible day.

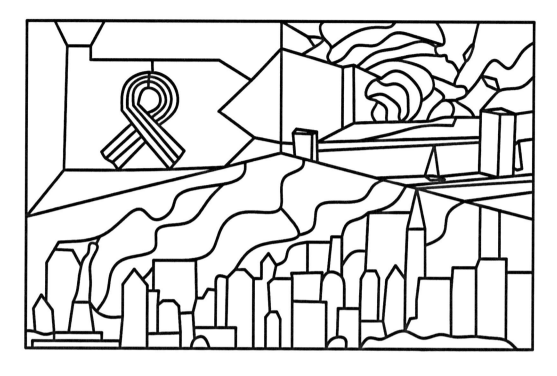

(Enlarge to 16 X 10)

Cabin in the Woods

(Enlarge to 16 x 20)

(Enlarge to 16 x 22)

Celtic Cross (extremely advanced)

(Enlarge to 18x18 or larger)

APPENDIX 2 - A SOUL'S JOURNEY INTO GLASS

Unlike most people, I started working in glass not because of some innate artistic talent or desire but as a form of healing. As a firefighter I saw too much hurt and pain in the six months beginning with 9-11. I saw more in those six months than I should have had to see in a lifetime. Earlier in my career I had gone to see an Employee Assistance Professional (counselor) to talk about stress. I was feeling a lot of stress in my job. I was also questioning the role of God in my life. He suggested that I try something creative. A creative outlet might let me relieve some of these emotions.

My first attempt was woodcarving. That was an unqualified failure. I can say right now that I was never meant to put chisel to wood, or Dremel to wood for that matter. Then, I thought about how I had loved looking at the stained glass windows in church and how much I had always wanted to learn about stained glass but I had shelved it away in the back of my brain. The only stained glass instructional studio and supply shop that I knew of had just closed down. But one day, on a country drive trying to lift my spirits out of depression, I saw a big red sign in a small strip mall. "STAINED GLASS STUDIO" the sign read. So I had to stop by. Sure enough it was a supply store, classroom and workshop all rolled into one. And it was run by three of the best ladies I know, Donna Darcy, Michelle Rikon & Diane Greene. They patiently taught me everything a beginner needed to know about stained glass. They also listened to me as I went through much psychological sorrow and trauma following 9-11 and beyond. But it was still just a hobby, an outlet for my emotions.

However, I was getting much better. In fact my skills with the glasscutters had grown to the point where I was almost as good as a professional. Then life threw me a curve ball. I was pulled from active duty because of excessive stress related to several incidents in which I was unable to rescue children from fires. I was at my breaking point. Then the county-appointed psychiatrist ruled that I had Post-Traumatic Stress Disorder and could never return to active duty. I had no idea what I was going to do with myself. I had anger inside me. I was angry at the Fire Department for sending me to the psychiatrist. I was angry with the doctor for ruling that I couldn't go back. I was angry with myself for being unable to save those lives. And I was angry with God for putting me in that situation. At that point I threw myself into working in glass.

It's amazing what working in glass 12 to 16 hours or more a day every day can do for one's skill level. I rapidly grew better at cutting, soldering and every other aspect of the craft. I even surpassed my mentors in skill. Then on June 14, 2002, I entered my first competition. It was a contest for patriotic projects held by Warner-Crivellaro. To my surprise I won 1st place. I couldn't believe it. It was that win that showed me where I was going in life. When God closes a door he opens a window. My window just happened to be made of stained glass.

Since that turbulent time stained glass has brought much joy to my life. The two September 11-related patterns have also helped bring emotional closure to my suffering as well. I still have PTSD. I still get sad a lot. I still have flashbacks. But I also have a safe place I can turn to in my workshop where I know that the only thing present is a thing of beauty.

I hope that this book has helped bring that beauty into your life as well.

Phillip C. McKee, III

APPENDIX 3 - DOWNLOAD SITES

You can download the GlassEye 2000 software as a free 30 day trial from this website:

http://www.mckeestainedglass.com/glasseye_bookdownload.php

Don't worry about it only being a 30 day trial. The good people at Dragonfly Software have set it up so you will still be able to access all of the patterns through GlassEye even after the trial period is over. However, you won't be able to save new patterns or modifications to existing patterns.

All of the patterns included in this book may also be downloaded in a .ZIP file. that includes both PDF and GlassEye formated versions, at this address:

http://www.mckeestainedglass.com/bookpatterns.php

Other Fine Books by Phillip C. McKee III Coming Soon:

Fuse It Or Lose It;

A Complete Textbook On Kilnforming Glass

&

Break It, Then Make It;

Mosaics For Beginners

Brought to you by

 CWS
Press

CPSIA information can be obtained at www.ICGtesting.com
Printed in the USA
LVOW09s1433010416

481783LV00008B/81/P